MAKING THE RIGHT FRIENDS
FOR TEEN GIRLS

Easy Workbook for Managing Anxiety, Controlling Emotions, and Building Self-Esteem to Form Friendships that Last

Illustrator: Rebecca Harrie

A FREE GIFT TO OUR READERS

FREE printable worksheets!

Share this book with others and have fun working through the quizzes and reflection sections together.

**To get exclusive access to this FREE Bonus, go to
friends.trueteenz.com/worksheets**

Or scan the QR code below!

TABLE OF CONTENTS

FORWARD

Making the Right Friends for Teen Girls is by far one of the best easy-to-read and informative self-help books I have come across. True Teenz provides detailed content and strategies on how to help support anxiety, emotional control and self-regulation, building friendships, identifying toxic relationships, and teaching social media etiquette.

In the ever-changing landscape of adolescence, teenage girls face a multitude of challenges as they navigate the complexities of relationships, self-discovery, and the world around them. Anxiety, self-doubt, and the struggle to forge meaningful connections are all too familiar to many young women. It is with great pleasure and empathy that I introduce this invaluable guide, written to support and inspire teenage girls as they journey through these formative years.

As a holistic psychotherapist, I practice many of these tools and coping strategies daily in my practice as a counselor with teen clients. I recognize the importance of addressing the whole person, rather than simply focusing on isolated symptoms or issues. This book provides great examples of how to move from feeling friendless, or anxious, to feeling connected and calm.

True Teenz gives detailed examples of the why's and how to's of anxiety, as well as step-by-step guidance on how to become an active listener. Additionally, Making the Right Friends for Teen Girls educates the adolescent population with clearly defined activities such as teaching cognitive distortions (a CBT technique), mindfulness tips (how to breathe and get in touch with your body), as well as communication support with initiating and maintaining conversations with new friends.

True Teenz implements therapeutic modalities such as CBT, DBT, mindfulness, and person-centered strategies in this helpful workbook. This thoughtful combination provides a comprehensive approach to help girls overcome anxiety and foster fulfilling friendships. The strategies and insights offered within these pages are rooted in the understanding that the mind, body, and spirit are interconnected, and that true healing and growth come from attending to each of these aspects.

During my years of practice, I have witnessed the transformative power of incorporating mindfulness, self-compassion, and emotional intelligence into the lives of my clients. By offering practical exercises and thought-provoking reflections, this book invites readers to cultivate these essential skills in their own lives. By fostering a deeper awareness of themselves and their emotions, girls will be better equipped to navigate the often tumultuous waters of adolescence and create authentic, lasting friendships.

One of the most important messages this book conveys is that each girl's journey is unique. There is no one-size-fits-all solution, and the path to self-discovery and connection may look different for everyone. I hope that the wisdom shared here will serve as a beacon, guiding each reader to uncover her own strengths, passions, and vulnerabilities. By embracing these facets of their individuality, girls can begin to redefine their relationships with themselves and others, ultimately finding the courage and resilience to create the life they deserve.

It is with great pride and admiration that I present this book to you. May it become a trusted companion on your journey, providing comfort, inspiration, and empowerment as you embark on the adventure of adolescence to adulthood. I highly recommend this book for any teen who is struggling with anxiety, social challenges, or emotional dysregulation. Remember that you are not alone and that with courage, self-compassion, and perseverance, you can overcome anxiety and create meaningful friendships that will enrich your life in countless ways.

Michelle Shlafman

Warmly,
Michelle Shlafman MS, LPC, ACS
Holistic Psychotherapist

"A friend is one who knows you and loves you just the same."

- Elbert Hubbard

Meredith Grey from Grey's Anatomy once said of best friend Cristina Yang,

'You're my person.'

Those words are enough to solidify any friendship, but finding a friend like this can be **extremely** daunting when anxiety and low self-esteem play such a massive role in your life.

When these feelings firmly reside within us, they can be challenging to talk about or express to others, such as family or friends.

To the outside world, everything seems fine. You get up, go to school, see the same people, and come home again. On the weekends, you might have a part-time job you go to, but mostly, you lead a contented life.

What could the problem be?

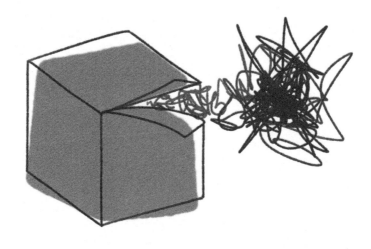

Anxiety lives in your head, rent-free.

It is unaware of your dreams and aspirations, as it coats your thoughts with negative assumptions that prevent you from taking risks. The more you try to fight it, the more problematic it is.

And boy, can it grow.

Thoughts that trap us can very quickly isolate us. This palpable loneliness makes us feel as though we don't have any genuine, uplifting connections, and any we actually want to make seem way out of reach, so we avoid trying.

The dull ache of rejection far outweighs the possibility of succeeding – so anxiety wins.

Rinse, repeat.

Have you ever sat with a group of people and observed their behavior? This isn't out of the ordinary for those who live with anxiety.

You know those times when there are a group of friends laughing and joking, living carefree? There could be several conversations going on at once, and the group is so in tune with the moment that it seems no problem, big or small, could affect them.

Except for you.

You might be more inclined to shuffle in your seat, glancing from person to person, wondering why you can't just let go. Let go, have fun, and laugh along when they do because you find it funny and not because you don't want to allow your thoughts to become your behavior.

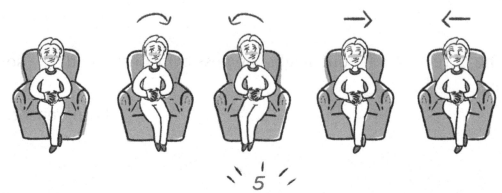

These times lead to a kind of emotional dysregulation that I want to help you overcome—turning those feelings of **sadness** and **frustration**
in social situations, into

practical

and

mindful

ways to allow you the escape from the vicious cycle of anxiety and fear.

You know it's unwanted, but you perhaps lack the coping mechanisms to get you to a place where making friends can come naturally to you.

I know that may seem impossible at the moment, but

page by page,
thought by thought,
and exercise by exercise,

you can rewire your mind to work in your favor.

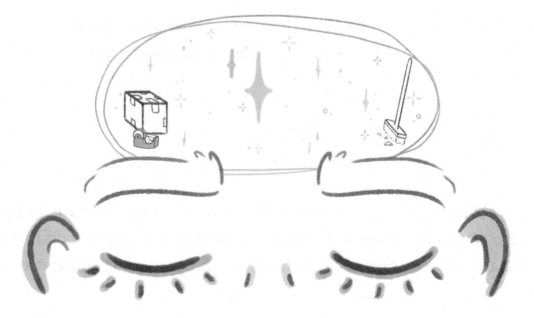

In doing so, you can determine what to do in those social situations and how to make genuine friends.

You can also learn to avoid **toxicity** by identifying the different ways people can bring their toxic behaviors into so-called friendships.

Being free from those people who only want to be your friend **conditionally** will lead you to a path of value and attract the right type of person for you. Your own person, or people, just like Meredith and Cristina.

Sometimes, it doesn't seem possible to feel empowered at your age. The years of adolescence come with the pressures of school alongside the obvious mind and body changes that happen to all girls and young women.

It is high time you get the support you **want** and **need** to create a smoother path into adulthood.

As this book aims to help relieve some of the pain of social anxiety in practical ways, it also gives you a chance to observe your own self-esteem and find ways to alleviate the negative traits that shift within you, sometimes uncontrollably.

Self-esteem is like a house, and this book is like the architectural plans.

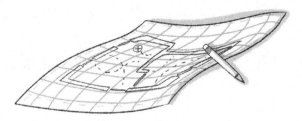

Brick by brick, you'll learn to take back the controls and live out the sense of belonging you wish you had but currently feel you lack.

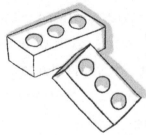

You'll build your confidence, layer by layer, and reveal your true potential, regardless of what you currently think.

There are various stories from girls who were once in your shoes in each chapter, and you can read about how they built their confidence and came out stronger.

Those moments you see yourself looking at someone and thinking, 'I would love to be friends with them,' will no longer be moments you allow to pass. Taking those leaps of faith gives you as many opportunities as possible to create those bonds.

Empowered people have and cherish empowered friendships.

Hockey player Wayne Gretzky nailed it when he was quoted saying:

'You miss 100% of the shots you don't take.'

This quote can be adapted to suit any situation, including yours. Missed opportunities do not build resilience or confidence, but they do kill hope.

This book aims to revive yours, offer you a vastly different outlook on friendship, and turn your insecurity around with advice, tips, and practical ways to overcome your fears. Consider it a pocket toolbox!

Ideally, you want to reach those goals and create a

harmonious   balance

in your life that allows you both the

freedom to learn

and the influence to be yourself.

Those outer forces, such as social media and image, are important and help shape how we identify, but the core beliefs we have and manage well give us room to grow and be our authentic selves.

This **can** and **will** be you.

Your task now is to start thinking about Wayne Gretzky's quote above and those **opportunities you don't want to miss** and use this book as your guide to getting there. You can work out the following:

- Practical steps to develop positive self-esteem/self-image
- Strategies for managing anxiety in social situations
- How to make genuine friendships
- How to identify toxic friendships and free yourself from them
- How to keep these friendships for the long haul

This book ended up in your hands for the sole purpose of offering you answers and solutions to all the problems you're carrying.

You have it because you have faith that **change is possible.**

I wish I had something like this when I was your age. It absolutely lacked in my life. Having that weight on my chest throughout those vital years of growing up was dismissed as momentary worries by so many, and I certainly never spoke about it with my friends at the time.

It was anxiety all along, and I never had anybody guide me through it until I trained myself out of it as a young adult. By then, there is so much more to unpack.

School would have its awful days, and I recall one particular girl I so wanted to befriend. She was so effortlessly cool without telling the world about it. She wasn't scared to sit up front in class and raise her hand. She was the best artist I ever knew, even to this day, and nothing was apparent that stopped me from talking to her. She wasn't unkind; I was just too afraid to be rejected.

Fast forward too many years, and I thought it was high time you had the 'something' I lacked. So much has changed in the short time since I was your age, so I am offering you something relevant for you today. Is this book an overnight fixer? Certainly not. Nothing that matters this much ever is. But that is the beauty of journeys of self-discovery. They take time, and in that time, we heal.

What matters is that you're here. You're tired of walking around on eggshells and want to make a change. Today is the start of you building your new house. Let's grab those plans and make a start.

After all, it's never too late!

Chapter 1

Why do I think this way? Anxiety overload.

From the outside, it's easy to think that somebody has got it all figured out, right? Without a care in the world, they go about their days pretending everything's OK and that nothing holds them back.

Since we tend not to walk around in t-shirts with '**I Have Anxiety**' memes on them, we assume we are alone. Is it the same for <u>you?</u>

That feeling of isolation creates even more anxious thoughts and feelings, which can lead to **SO** much frustration.

I wanted to introduce you to anxiety in this first chapter. It's a little like introducing a friend to another friend, except instead of, 'Hi, this is Stacey, and she is an art major in college,' it's more,

> 'Hi, this is anxiety, and it can be an incredible pain in the **you-know-what**, but here's how the two of you can get along.'

It can make us feel powerless when we give way to anxiety or fear. Sitting with it instead of fighting may not make it disappear, but it does give you a chance not to allow it to take over your life.

It can be done!

What is anxiety?

You might be thinking of a few choice words at this time.

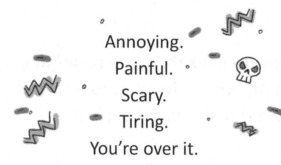

Annoying.
Painful.
Scary.
Tiring.
You're over it.

Those are all valid, but let's take a deeper look into what anxiety is and why our bodies create it.

Imagine you are on a camping trip with your family. You've set up your tents in a small circle, and in the middle lies a warm campfire where you are cooking some fresh fish.

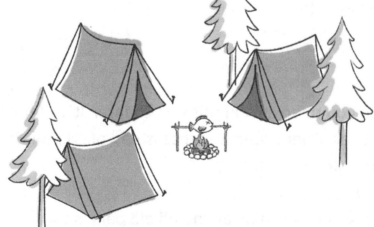

You're having a wonderful time without a care in the world when suddenly, you hear a rustling in the nearby trees.

It's a mountain lion!

Stop there.

What do you think happens to your body?

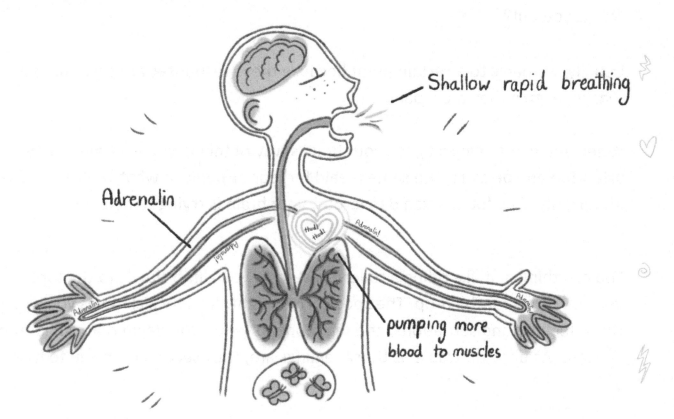

Shallow rapid breathing

Adrenalin

pumping more
blood to muscles

Your nervous system will spring into action. The hormone adrenalin will flood into your bloodstream. Your body is now on high alert. Your heartbeat gets faster, sending more blood to your muscles. Your breathing will become rapid and shallow, allowing you to absorb more oxygen. You feel way more alert.

All these changes occur instantly so we can get ourselves out of dangerous situations.

Our bodies are amazing machines. They serve us well, and in situations of actual danger or threat, anxiety and panic can be helpful, believe it or not!

What, though, if there is no lion?
What if there is no danger?

What if you have a test or if you find yourself in an unfamiliar situation that freaks you out?

Usually, we panic to a certain point because these responses are there for a reason, even if they are a pain.

When you feel any anxiety, it's your brain's way of telling you it's time to **pay attention** and be alert. The same is said for fear or panic. If what you're doing is important, stressful, or even dangerous, your brain is trying to help you.

You can think of it like riding a roller-coaster. As you climb slowly to the top, you're waiting for the drop. The speed. The height. Anxiety kicks in as you await those feelings and sensations, and fear appears when you begin that exhilarating descent. As uncomfortable as those feelings are, they serve a purpose: to help you.

We all know anxiety doesn't work that way. Anxiety is the sheer terror that something terrible will happen, with our brains being our arch enemy. When the anxiety mood hits you, your body will set off what's known as the 'fight or flight' response, as in the lion scenario.

What is fight or flight?

If we go back to that camping trip and think more about fight or flight, we can begin to see how each one could play out.

Firstly, there is fight. Your heart is pumping, and you've been given the energy and focus to put your fists up and physically fight the lion. Would you want to? I mean... it's a lion... but your body is giving you everything it can for you to give it a solid go.

Then there is flight. We see the lion. We run. It's that simple. We must get away from it before it chews us up and spits us out. That is my favorite option, even if it means sacrificing my delicious fish.

Your body, at this time, goes a little like this:

1. **Pale or flushed skin** – The surface areas of the body doesn't get as much blood, as it's too busy in other areas like muscles, legs, brain, and arms.

2. **Trembling** – As your muscles tense, it can cause shaking or trembling.

3. **Rapid breathing** – More breathing, more oxygen.

Anxiety and the relaxation response

Having anxiety can confuse the fight or flight response, making us think something is wrong when in fact, there is nothing wrong.

This type of stress can help you do better in situations where you feel the pressure to do well, like school, where you may not experience something life-threatening, but the fight or flight response still plays a vital role in your survival. It does this by gearing you up to do something stressful so that you can **survive the moment.**

The good news is there is a solution to the fight or flight response known as
'the relaxation response.'

The relaxation response reverses stress in a really cool way. When the body is no longer in perceived danger, our automatic nervous system returns to normal, like our body's 'off switch.'

What you'll notice about your body is that:

- Blood pressure mellows
- Heart rate slows down
- Hormone levels balance out
- Your digestion system settles

Consider it like a huge sigh of relief.

Goals, right?

There will come a time later on when we will look at strategies for firing up this response. Right now, you may feel like that just ain't gonna happen, but it will. Have faith!

When anxiety and fear disrupt your life
The anxiety cycle

Fortunately, we do not attend daily camping holidays, with endless lions wanting to attack us. We are not savages.

This is where anxiety comes in because it survives based alone on the constant worry of your worst nightmare becoming your reality. The constant worry leads to attention given to those potential threats, with your body trying to see if, or how, it will cope with them.

When you notice your anxious symptoms, you immediately turn to the narrative that you can't cope with the situation, so you become more anxious. **Fun, huh?**

This is the start of the vicious cycle of anxiety. This cycle is frequent and ongoing and is often triggered by a single thought of something or someone.

It is the type of cycle that disrupts everything, as our imagination creates a bunch of scenarios that we may encounter in the future.

This is where our minds create **negative** outcomes, as anxiety rarely gives us a positive look into our future.

We all have abilities to think about how different experiences may turn out. Anxiety thinks the bad stuff without any of it even happening, and it is **super** annoying and disruptive.

We activate our nervous system, that alarm response, with thought alone. This cycle can result in us avoiding certain things,

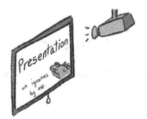 such as a presentation at school, by pretending to be ill.

Another one could be not going out with friends or to events because you assume something horrible will happen.

Those choices we make interfere with our ability to find meaning and positivity for ourselves in the long run, but getting out of that vicious anxiety cycle is tough and does involve some work.

In addition, anxiety and fear disrupt our lives so much that we forget to live in the **here and now.**

Let's say you are returning to school after being off for a week with the flu. You walk into class to see your classmates all laughing and joking together. None of them have noticed you, and your stomach turns to knots. Thoughts suddenly begin appearing:

'What if they hate me?'
'Are they talking about me?'
'Do they even care that I was sick?'
'What if they won't let me sit with them?'

The anxiety within you wakes up, and those fight-or-flight feelings start to kick in.

Suddenly those questions are replaced with assumptions:

'They hate me.'
'They are talking about me.'
'They don't care that I was sick.'
'I bet they won't let me sit with them. I'll have to sit on my own.'

Um, table for 1 at the crazy table, anyone?

Your classmates are just hanging out and spending time together chatting; seeing that and *believing* that are two different things.

Let's take a quick look at that vicious cycle so you can see how it manifests detrimental outcomes:

Long-term: Anxiety kicking in physically and mentally. Loss of confidence about coping and more worry. These create an increased use of safety behaviors.

Anxiety.

-

You scan for danger. You start to feel even worse, and everything is more intense—attention narrows and shifts to you.

-

Escape or avoidance? Help!

-

Short term: Relief. You've calmed.

-

Rinse. Repeat.

The cycle is tiring and manifests a great deal of anxiety within us.

How anxiety manifests

Whether or not you have been medically diagnosed with anxiety, you are still experiencing it in all its glory. There are many ways it festers inside us, and you may find one or two of these relevant to you.

Avoidance

You may avoid school, sleepovers, or public events through fear of something embarrassing happening, feeling out of control, or getting asked something you don't like. The list is endless and exhausting, making you want to just curl up and watch Netflix in your room.

Going places on your own

As scary as it seems, even with familiar places, you decline any opportunity to go out and be alone. Girl, bye!

Sleeping troubles

The one time you want to lie down in a quiet room and gather some quality rest is usually when your brain wakes up and gives you a dozen worst-case scenarios that keep you wide awake. Over time, it can cause a severe decline in your mental health. Good sleep is the ultimate link to good health.

Physical symptoms

Developing regular headaches and stomach aches or feeling sick are your body's way of telling you that there is anxiety within you. It's like a sponge holding onto water. It becomes dense and heavy and can no longer function as it's designed to because nobody is ridding it of its contents. It's the same with you if you hold onto all your baggage without finding ways to breathe and appreciate the moment. There might even be muscle tension in your upper body.

Eating troubles

Whether you eat for comfort or refuse through sheer nausea and panic, it is likely what you eat can be affected at some point. In turn, not getting the proper nutrition can also negatively impact our bodies and mind. If we aren't fuelling correctly, we don't perform properly.

Fatigue

Because, let's be honest, constantly battling with your thoughts every single day is exhausting!

Sweating

As if it isn't hard enough being a teenager and having to face growing up and ever-changing hormones, you'll also be inclined to sweat as you panic, likely leading to more sweating. Cringe.

In social settings, anxious teenagers, just like you, may appear dependent, withdrawn, or uneasy.

You may seem as though you're holding back or possibly overly emotional. Being preoccupied with worries about losing control or concerns that aren't very realistic about how competent you are socially can also affect you.

As these symptoms hit you like a ton of bricks, and because you are going through so many adolescent changes, you'll likely want to run away and may appear majorly shy to others.

Suddenly those things you'd usually enjoy go right out the window. **Deleting social media accounts can occur as a result;** if you have ever been so overwhelmed you've deleted your TikTok or ghosted your Instagram, I hear you!

How social anxiety changes the way you think about everything

Social anxiety disorder (SAD) has a way of coloring in areas of your life that should remain grey. It takes something that would normally be totally lit and colors it with a vibrant shade of red. That color creates this warning in your head that something is wrong.

SAD is linked with **thinking negative things about yourself** and being incredibly self-critical. With a lot of research, people now know **it can really alter your identity.**

Your basic thoughts might include:

1. I'm making a fool of myself.
2. I can't control my anxiety.
3. I hate myself.
4. I look stupid.
5. I'm so awkward.

And so on.

A little like the scenario after being ill and returning to school above, your mind goes to all the awful things and never makes room for the good.

Eventually, these types of negative thoughts affect how you feel about yourself and determine the choices you make as a result.

What about how you think about others?

Those who don't suffer from anxiety view new people as potential friends, whereas you may respond to new faces with fear and detachment and flat-out ignore them.

> 'They will probably hate me. I'm not interesting
> enough to be friends with. I'm so shy and awkward.
> Why even bother?'

Others might see friends as comfort blankets to make you feel better and always have your back.

There is the problem of others treating you based on your view of them. If you see them as someone to be **fearful of and avoid, they will be less likely to approach you** and want to hang out and may eventually give up.

Your body language alone in these situations would be enough to steer potential friends off, and guess what? They have then become the very thing you thought them to be, but only toward you.

In some warped way, your mind and thoughts about others have given you exactly what you assumed them to be.

When you view the world, do you see it as an exciting or scary place? Is it filled with opportunity or dread? The chances are, it may not be what you want it to be. With these types of thoughts, I bet your world feels safer. But with such a **small world**, you have equally as **small opportunities**, and some people view that as a good thing because it means less can go wrong.

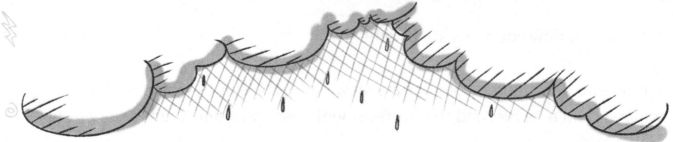

Anxiety shows the future as a collection of clouds. Sometimes there is a risk for SAD leading to depression because you spend each day feeling things will never change or improve. This will reaffirm your belief that you can't do something about it, which is not a great vibe.

Past social events play a role in how your social anxiety can develop. It can be that perhaps something bad happened once, so you assume it will be that way each and every time. It's as if your memories are haunting you. Anxiety is viewed as a constant threat.

'What if I go and have a panic attack?'
'What if everyone notices?'

Ask yourself if you can regularly smile and chat with your classmates or if you feel open and relaxed to others. Is your mind clear and sharp? The chances are not, and this is because social anxiety zaps you of your energy. Every time you panic, your battery life goes down.

You just can't find the charger.

Avoidance behaviors

Anxiety can lead to things we do or don't do to make it go away. In the long run, these behaviors can prove problematic because the more we try to escape something, the more often they don't go away.

You might:

- Drop a class if there is too much attention on talking in public.
- Fail to show up to events that cause anxiety.

If you have to go somewhere you are dreading; you might escape early or hide in the bathroom instead of making yourself seen and heard. You could avoid eye contact or talk as little as possible to avoid any attention on you. This is known as **'partial avoidance.'**

So when we adopt these avoidance behaviors, what are we telling ourselves? We are permitting ourselves to be comforted by walking away from what troubles us. We, in turn, encourage the cycle by maintaining these symptoms and allowing anxiety to win.

When you think there isn't a solution, you'll find one in the form of exposure. Whatever it is that causes the fear will be what you need to face in order for it to go away.

Here is a classic example from Sarah, 13

'It's easier said than done to stop worrying. This bridge is so tall and narrow in my town that I just avoided walking over it. I used to just stand and wait for ages to cross the road instead.

Eventually, I did it. I just kept thinking, 'fear is just an emotion' on a loop in my mind. I was literally freaking out, but I knew deep down I didn't even have anything to worry about. What was my worry? I just needed my brain to know that!

I'm glad I did it.'

How anxiety affects relationships

Anxiety can negatively impact so much of your life, including your social life. It can affect how you approach challenges and communicate and connect with friends. Let's look at some signs of anxiety in a relationship (friendship and romantic).

Signs of anxiety in relationships

You may think, 'oh yup, that's me,' with these signs of anxiety in a relationship:

- Fearing that the other person may like other people better
- Worrying that the other person is lying
- Being worried that the other person may cheat
- Worrying that your anxiety will kill the relationship
- Overthinking every phone call, text, comment, or conversation
- Pushing people away to avoid rejection
- Avoiding relationships altogether

These signs can often lead to further problems for those who suffer from anxiety, and those experiencing it may respond by being too **avoidant** or too **dependent**. Either way – these feelings can take a toll.

Dependence

Having anxiety can create a strong desire for closeness to friends or partners. You might constantly reach out for support or reassurance rather than finding it on the inside.

You might:

- Fear rejection
- Seek out constant communication
- Plan for worst-case scenarios
- 'Like' and 'comment' on every single post
- Overthink your interactions
- Be clingy

Avoidance

Way down on the other end of the spectrum, you might avoid relationships altogether. The mere thought alone of creating closeness with another person makes you cringe.

'What if I am rejected?'

Does that sound familiar?

Avoiding negative emotions by not opening up or being vulnerable may make you think you're trying to protect yourself. Still, from my experience and many others, it only leads to feelings of isolation and loneliness, which just worsens things.

Common anxiety triggers

Socially, we can find all kinds of triggers that fire up feelings of panic and anxiety, including:

- How you're perceived
- Your body
- Public speaking
- Speaking in front of peers

Anxiety is a self-esteem destroyer, but now that you have more knowledge about it, there are many ways to help yourself the same way other girls did when they were your age.

It's time now to turn to stories from girls who were recently in your shoes.

Before the end of each chapter and the workbook section, you can read about what they went through, just like you.

As promised, each chapter will provide you with the experience of someone once your age. You'll know you can do the same in learning what they went through and how they successfully overcame their anxieties.

Meet Jessica, 19

Inspired by the following quote:

> *"Rejection triggers my anxiety and depression. Once I learn how to choose myself and be completely validated by that choice, I'll put the trigger in my hands and not in the hands of others."*
> *-Lizzo.*

'I remember starting high school so well. I transferred there with all my friends and was so excited.

The morning we got to the main hall, 200 of us were led in and given the name of our new class. I sat and watched my friends go off together in groups of at least 3.

I remained seated, looking around at more people I didn't recognize and less and less people that I did.

Suddenly, it was my turn. I was called to the front, with 29 others. Some I sort of knew, but most were strangers. They seemed to all know each other, which was the worst thing.

I felt that feeling in my stomach like it had been twisted into knots. My heart began to beat faster, and I wanted to just run out the door and all the way home. I knew my mom would be there, and she would comfort me.

I stayed and tried to smile at the other girls.

It was the **worst** time!

Eventually, we were led to class and separated from anybody we knew already (lucky me) to sit with somebody we didn't know. It was the school's way of getting us to meet and chat, all in the same boat.

It helped a little, but come break and lunch, I found my friends again, who, of course, were all laughing and joking because they'd spent the morning together.

Over time, I made new friends, but I will never forget how fearful I felt that first morning not knowing anyone and having to jump so far out of my comfort zone.

It wasn't easy, but looking back, I just wanted to carry on being

myself

so that I could make the right friends, not just any friends.

My tip would be to take it a day at a time and know that you are not alone.

Journaling helped me and may help you too, as I was able to reflect on my experiences and seek ways to challenge my negative thoughts. Always be true to yourself.'

Now it's time to make it 'work, work, work, work, work'!

The first action step in this section is identifying what sets your anxiety off. This is about guiding you through your specific triggers and reflecting on past situations that have caused you anxiety.

What situations have you been in triggering those feelings of panic and worry? Perhaps you remember feeling them at school.

_____

_____

_____

_____

_____

_____

Other triggers could be:

- Joining a new club or group
- Being invited to a party
- Realizing your best friend is not at school and worrying that you'll have nobody to chat with
- Starting a new school after moving
- Liking somebody either platonically or romantically but feeling unsure how to start a conversation

Action step: Identify avoidance behaviors

In looking at the situations that cause you anxiety and identifying what you do during those times, you can begin to see patterns.

What do you do to avoid something that makes you anxious?

( ) Do you avoid eye contact?

( ) You may find a way to leave the room or make excuses for yourself.

( ) Do you fake an illness so you can go home?

( ) _____

_____

_____

_____

_____

_____

Pick one from above, and that one will be your project for the week.

 When you notice yourself doing it, consciously stop and recognize the action.

Reflection: Imagine you wake up tomorrow and your anxiety has *completely* disappeared. It might be hard to think about it, but say it happened. How would your life be different? Try your best to think of and list three specific examples.

1.

2.

3.

Pros and cons worksheet activity

Below is a worksheet that can help you examine the pros and cons of addressing your social anxiety. These activities can help open your eyes and let you look beyond the smaller picture to see more of what's happening *behind* the scenes.

We often get these magical, eye-opening moments that feel like piecing together a jigsaw puzzle, so I hope this sheet can start to do that for you.

Step 1: Write down the thought you are having about your social anxiety. This is known as the problem statement.
For example: Should I try and make friends with the new girl?

Problem statement: _____

_____

Step 2: Take a moment (10, 20, 30 minutes) and list all the pros (the positives) and all the cons (the negatives) for your statement. What can you think of that sets your worries off, or can you think of anything good that could come from your problem statement?

Step 3: Once all pros and cons have been listed, go through each one and write down a value from 1 to 10, with 1 being not important at all and 10 being extremely important.

Step 4: Add up each column. Whichever sum is larger will give you the answer to the problem statement.

Give it a go! You might be surprised.

Pros	Weight	Cons	Weight
Sum:			

How do you feel?

The first step to overcoming your anxiety is to **understand** it. It isn't easy because it involves unraveling layers of yourself that may make you feel uncomfortable, especially if we have kept ourselves protected from the root cause.

Spending time educating yourself on your experiences can make your anxious experiences less scary because you know what's happening. That **familiarity** can really help you in the future.

While that doesn't mean it'll be easy to overcome them, you can go forward knowing it is possible.

Like anything, it just takes time.

Chapter 2

Who am I? Identifying your strengths.

After looking at your own anxiety, I wanted to introduce this chapter as a way to challenge the one thing that can encourage your worries – your self-esteem.

It can be difficult and super uncomfortable to admit that things we don't like about ourselves lead to low self-esteem. It is painful to reflect, right? It means we have to be a bit vulnerable.

You may be thinking of several things you wish were different about yourself. Don't forget, we all do that to an extent – that's all part of being human.

But when we focus on all the things we don't like, we miss out on so much of the **good stuff**!

Through this next section, you'll see that it's OK to be vulnerable and it's OK to like yourself.

What is self-esteem?

Imagine you are carrying a bag that can hold maybe 200 gold coins. Each coin would represent a part of yourself that you like. You might have a coin for how kind you are or a coin for your gorgeous hair. If you had a bag right now, how heavy would it be? How many coins would be inside?

Self-esteem doesn't come from likes and followers.
Self-esteem is all about how you value yourself - your personal worth.
You may refer to it as self-respect, self-value, or self-worth.
However you perceive it, it is all about you.

The key elements of self-confidence include:

1. Self-consciousness
2. Feelings of security
3. Sense of identity
4. Knowing you're competent
5. Sense of belonging

Why self-esteem is important

It's important to remember that self-esteem affects your overall well-being hugely. It isn't just how you treat yourself; it reflects in your relationships, decision-making, and emotional and physical health.

It also influences your motivation because if you have a healthy and positive view of yourself, you'll be able to understand your potential and will be far more likely and inspired to take on new challenges.

The impacts of having healthy and unhealthy self-esteem vary, so I want you to look at the different points carefully.

Healthy self-esteem:

- A strong understanding of who you are and what you like
- The ability to maintain healthy relationships with others because of the healthy relationship you have with yourself
- Expectations that are realistic and appropriate
- A good understanding of your own needs and the ability to express them
- Knowing what you want

Unhealthy self-esteem:

- Less secure in your abilities
- Doubting the decisions you make
- Unmotivated to try new things thinking you might fail
- Issues with expressing your needs leading to failing relationships
- Low confidence, feeling unlovable and worthless

There is a major difference, isn't there? Do you recognize yourself in any of those descriptions?

Do you have healthy self-esteem? If you do something well and that particular thing is noticed by somebody else, do you feel that huge positivity surge? Do you speak without fear of rejection?

Those who value their worth are often able to separate their feelings from facts and not take things personally, with a good level of appreciation for the other person.

People with healthy self-esteem see negative emotions such as anger, fear, and guilt and work with them so they can determine the reason for, and source, of those emotions.

They dance to the beat of their drum, tend not to follow the masses, and know that the past belongs behind them, <u>living for now.</u>

Those who experience unhealthy or low self-esteem often focus only on the negative parts of life. They lack boundaries, being too inviting or not friendly enough. There may be a lot of negative self-talk and self-hatred, or they may view their body image negatively.

Sound familiar?

Some people with low self-esteem think that other people are better than them in many ways, or they are obsessed with perfection and feel that they aren't good enough.

They might find it tricky to express their needs or rely on everyone else to do it for them. This can lead to poor decisions that prove they could have better self-esteem. They may find themselves constantly apologizing or feeling guilty for literally the tiniest thing.

Accepting compliments through gritted teeth – because you just don't think you're awesome enough to deserve them (you totally are!)

How self-esteem affects our quality of life

Are we living the **quality of life** we deserve? If we pay attention to how we feel, it's likely a big no!

The good thing about healthy self-esteem is that it gives us a sense of security in our lives. It's that feeling of everything being OK and that whatever troubles come your way, you have the tools to deal with them effectively, without feeling as though anything happening in the world is a reflection of your negative mind.

Of course, there is also the beauty of having less stress in your life – which is always a freaking awesome bonus!

People with low self-esteem see themselves, the world, and their future more negatively and critically. Those constant questions you go over and over will eventually reduce your confidence and kill any hopes or dreams.

The one thing with low self-esteem is that it seems never-ending. It's as if nothing will ever change, and that vicious cycle I mentioned in the previous chapter can also be relevant here. If you have struggled with self-confidence your entire life, it's hard to believe you can ever feel differently.

And before you totally freak out and feel alone in this, 7 in 10 girls believe they aren't good enough or don't measure up in some way, shape, or form. This includes their looks, how they perform at school, and relationships with friends and family. 7 in 10!

So, the next time you're in class and looking around and feeling as if you are the only one going through the pitfalls of poor self-image and low self-esteem, you really aren't.

Self-esteem is generally fuelled by our inner voices, like what we tell ourselves day-to-day. Some people are lucky enough to have a cheerful voice going on inside, but others are not.

In fact, you probably know that your inner voice can be flat-out mean sometimes, which impacts how you view yourself. Over a long period of time, it crushes us.

What is negative thinking?

We all engage in negative thinking from time to time; there's no mistake about that. Here's the thing, though. When your mind *constantly* travels to negative places *automatically*, it can destroy your mental health and increase those anxious feelings we discussed earlier.

Negative thinking (or negative self-talk) is like a nasty running inner voice that gets stronger over time. It becomes very difficult to control when it is let loose within the mind. Depressing, huh!

These thoughts are known as 'cognitive distortions' – and if I give you a few examples, you will begin to understand what that means:

- 'I just failed that English paper. I'm not good at school. I may as well just quit.'

- 'My teacher wants to see me after class. I've done something wrong, per usual.'

There are **10 types of cognitive distortion thinking patterns**, and I want to go through them with you so that they can help you understand more about yourself and the way you think.

1. Polarized thinking/all-or-nothing thinking

This black-or-white thinking happens when people think in total extremes. Something is either *amazing* or **terrible**, with nothing in between...

This doesn't give much time for the mind to find reason in different situations. Like if you don't do as well on a test as you normally would, you're more likely to think how much of a failure you are instead of shrugging it off as a bad day and promising yourself you'll do better next time. It's super unrealistic to think this way because, most of the time, reality exists somewhere between the two extremes.

2. Overgeneralization

This type of thinking comes from the outcome of **one** thing set to mean the same across the board.

For example, you could have a fallout with a classmate and conclude that this will happen with any future potential friends and that you're a horrible person. It's the idea that if you have a negative experience on one occasion, you develop the belief that will be the case forever. A rather terrible destiny!

3. Catastrophizing

Do you ever dread or fear the **worst in all scenarios?** This is the case for catastrophizing. It is a really chaotic way of thinking, as worries quickly escalate based on your thoughts, building up crazy, imaginary, and very negative narratives.

Say you call in sick at your weekend job because you aren't well,

then worry that it will lead to a job loss,

And *then*

you won't be able to afford to go to the concert you're saving for or for college in the future...

That!

Some people think overthinking means overreacting, but they and you shouldn't think this way. These thoughts can stem from when you were really little as a response to what was happening around you.

4. Personalization

One of the most common cognitive distortions. Taking things personally, even when something is not connected to or caused by you, can land your mind in a whole heap of trouble!

You might find that you **blame yourself for circumstances that aren't your fault** or if you think you have been intentionally excluded or targeted.

This could be times like somebody who usually says hi to you one day and then does not the next. 'What did I do wrong?' may be the first thought, without rationally thinking they just didn't see you or are having a bad day.

5. Mind reading

Mind reading and empathy are *very* different, so to claim you know what somebody else is thinking, especially when that claim negatively impacts you, is a common cognitive distortion.

It's never a good idea to assume what's going on in someone else's mind because you aren't necessarily working with all the facts.

It might be that a classmate you like is talking to a new girl in class, and you think that means you're being ignored because she finds you boring. This type of thinking leads to a real spike in anxiety.

You're so not boring!

6. Mental filtering

Another distorted thought pattern is where you ignore everything positive and focus exclusively on the negatives.

It's like having a negative mental filter, and not only is it unhelpful, but it's wrong! You could have had a great day, but one lousy reply to your latest snap streak can lead to extreme focus on that one moment, disregarding all the good.

And hey, your Snapchats rock!

7. Discounting the positive

<u>Disregarding the good stuff</u> in your life as luck or a fluke can sometimes be people's way of **assuming** nothing good *ever* happens to them on purpose.

You might think you're doing OK because you're not necessarily ignoring the positives, but you're instead downplaying your abilities by innocently yet incorrectly thinking you can't do good things on purpose.

It's like coming in first place on field day and laughing to yourself that everyone else must have had a bad day for you to win.

Is it possible that you were just better than everybody else at this event?

8. 'Should' statements

Sometimes, people think of what '**should**' or '**ought**' to be said or done, which is another cognitive distortion.

It's like assuming what you're doing at one moment is not justified and should be exchanged for something more useful.

You might be at home, homework finished and just catching up with some music or TV, and in walk your parents, and you immediately feel like you should be doing something.

Whatever happened to just being OK with chillaxing?!

9. Emotional reasoning

Emotional reasoning is a way of thinking that you're always right. Is what you're feeling based on any hard evidence? It's important to weigh that **before** you assume that your thoughts and feelings are facts, because if they are negative, you'll feel negative.

For example, you might think everyone hates you. That's a bold statement and one that is likely not factual, but if you feel it and manifest those feelings and thoughts enough, you'll spin the narrative to be true.

10. Labeling

If you could describe yourself using one word, what would it be?
Firstly, the mistake you may be making is assuming that your entire identity, or anyone else's, can be whittled down to one word.

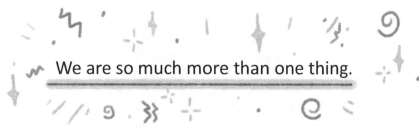

We are so much more than one thing.

We embrace *so* many beliefs and morals, and we have *so* much personality that a common cognitive distortion such as labeling should be banned! However, it isn't, leading to a great deal of misunderstanding and underestimation.

So how do we fix these distortions?

Fixing common cognitive distortions

The following exercises will help you manage and control irrational and negative thoughts.

There may be one you like to do more than the other, and that's alright, but try them all at least once and see how they feel for you.

Please give them a go!

Examine the evidence

The next time you feel your mind creating negative assumptions, I want you to picture someone you admire a lot. It might be a parent, a teacher, or even a celebrity! (What's up, Zendaya!)

Imagine them folding their arms and looking at you with a slight head tilt and saying, 'really?!' in a dry, sarcastic manner. They don't believe you; why should you believe yourself?

Let that be your prompt for looking at the evidence presented and the beginning of your being able to separate fact from fiction.

Double standard method

Think about how you would react if a sibling or cousin came to you with the thoughts that you're having. Would you agree with them and say, 'yeah, actually, you do suck, and you are going to fail in school and life.'

The drama - no!

You'd be uplifting and encouraging them to think more positively. You'd help them out of their rut, right? Try thinking about that the next time you are stuck in yours.

Thinking in shades of grey

It's time to introduce some shades of grey! That black-or-white thinking we talked about earlier? It's about knowing that all-or-nothing thoughts are, well, dumb and ***totally* unrealistic**!

There is a whole field of opportunity between black and white to explore, and the uncomfortable realization that something in there may work in your favor will be new to you.

Pause when you need to, and try to reframe those thoughts. It's like throwing rocks into a flowing river to try to steer the path of the water in a different direction. One rock or one thought at a time, and you can do the same for your mind.

Experimental method

Before making conclusions about yourself, you can start to **ask questions**. We find our answers by testing things rather than jumping straight to the evaluation. It is about seeking the facts. So, the next time something doesn't go entirely your way, think about times prior that it has.

Survey method

We get answers by asking other people's opinions who are in a similar situation. This can help us consider whether our thoughts and attitudes are true and realistic.

Are you a failure because of **one** mishap? Misfortunes happen to us all, even the most successful and happy people on the planet. Even Hailey Bieber! It's about being **objective**, not **subjective**, and learning that our thoughts are not factual.

Sum of its parts

When you next think you're a failure, consider a giant chocolate cake with the cake representing you. Take that one moment where things didn't go according to plan, and imagine cutting a small slither from the cake, then take it out. What's left?

Literally, all the cake is left. One mistake doesn't consume your entire cake.

Opposite threes

Each time you find yourself generalizing, think of three opposite thoughts to the situation. For example, when you think, 'I never do anything right,' try pointing your attention to identifying three scenarios where you have been

efficient, accurate, successful.

Try not to assume you've never been any of those things because, girl, you have.

Semantic method

It's time to give your vocabulary a shake-up! Instead of using words like 'I should' (which we all agree is not helpful), try 'It would be nice if....'

We all need to stop 'should-ing' all over everything. It leaves us with feelings of guilt and shame, so throw in some new words that will eventually give way to new thoughts.

Definitions

Nothing is ever as it seems, and labels are no different. Defining yourself one way, when there are so many, is a way of **shutting down the learning about the rest of yourself and your capabilities.**

Think of yourself in a dark house with just one small window open. The place will still be pretty dark, and ultimately you want a light, comforting home, right? So, start opening more windows. Let that light in!

Re-attribution

Rather than solely blaming yourself for every little thing, it's time to lighten your load. It's about looking objectively at the *bigger picture* and thinking about what you couldn't control that played a role in these downer days.

It isn't about blame shifting or pointing fingers; it's about realizing that **not everything is 100% our fault all of the time.**

Cost-benefit analysis

When you think of a thought that is unhelpful to you, try to ask yourself,

'How does this thought help me, and how does it hurt me?'

You can work with and fight those moments where you try to talk yourself out of uncomfortable situations, which can be a game changer. Maybe there is a school dance you're going to, but you're dreading making a fool of yourself. How is it helpful to think that, and how is it hurtful?

How to deal with self-doubt and low self-esteem

It takes some practice, and I know it always seems easier said than done, but there is magic in creating time to reflect and shutting the noise of the world off while you focus on yourself.

Here are some great ways to deal with self-doubt and low self-esteem:

Be kind to yourself

Know that challenging unkind thoughts about yourself is hard work, but it takes a consistent amount of time to see changes. Don't be hard on yourself for falling back into old thoughts. Just try to remember new ways to feel better, implementing them as much as possible.

Try to recognize positives

Celebrate when things go *right*, and enjoy your extraordinary moments! If people are praising you, it's because they have good reason to.

Writing them down in a journal can help you reflect on your strengths.

Build a support network

Talking to someone you trust is critical during times of negative thinking. Focusing on the positive relationships you have can help you feel good about yourself.

Set mini challenges

You can start a new hobby or revive an old one. If you have any small goal, do it! What about that TikTok dance you've been dying to learn or binging a Netflix show? Whatever brings you joy and makes you feel good.

Take control of your thoughts

Not freaking out when you have a negative thought will feel a little awkward at first. It'll be all you know to react a certain way, but if you can remember how thoughts, and how you view things, come from your negative mind and not from facts, it will help control them later.

When you concentrate on all the fantastic things in your life and learn to celebrate all the good stuff, you'll start to **build** your self-esteem.

Practice self-compassion

Catch yourself throwing around negative self-talk and replace it with something sweet you'd say to a friend in the same situation.

Also – and it's a biggy – you've got to avoid comparing yourself to others. If someone you know has double the amount of Instagram followers as you, it isn't because they're better, prettier, or have more things going on in their lives. They're probably bots! We're all gifted and unique in our own crazy and kind ways, including you.

Think about what you want and be clear about it. Your needs and wants will come thick and fast if you're kind to yourself.

Practice _positive_ self-talk

Breaking news:
negative self-talk is the <u>worst</u> thing for stress.

I'm not talking about the odd time we feel negatively; I'm talking constant, needless crushing of positivity.

One powerful way to stop this is to literally catch yourself doing it.

"Stop!"

If you want to say it out loud, go ahead, but even saying it on the inside will stop the cycle you've created and spin a better outcome over time.

An excellent way to be more positive is to replace negative statements that you spin to yourself by:

<u>Using milder wording</u> – stop with the 'terrible' and replace it with 'not so great,' or 'hate' with 'don't like.'
<u>Negative to neutral or positive</u> – Thinking about those last-minute canceled plans doesn't have to be sad. Hey, isn't the new season of your favorite show on Hulu? ...exactly!
<u>Self-limiting statements to questions</u> – We've all been there! 'This is impossible!' needs to get in the bin and be replaced with, 'how is this possible?' Don't give up; _give in_ to the possibilities.

Practice <u>positive</u> affirmations

These are super effective and help you manage stress and anxiety in your daily struggles. So many people use them, and they are really cool to write down and read when you are out and need a <u>pick-me-up</u>.

Firstly, learn what negative thoughts you have and when they creep up on you so you can slay them as soon as they enter your mind.

'My hair is disgusting today, and everyone will laugh at me'

can soon become,

'My hair looks different than usual. I might put it up and rock a ponytail.'

You can use general affirmations, too, to get you through 'those' types of days, such as:

- Anxiety isn't dangerous, just super uncomfortable. I'll be OK, though.
- The words in my head are so unhealthy. I'm being negative.
- I feel anxious, but so what? It's just a feeling. It will pass.

It's taking something big and turning it into something **small** and **manageable**.

Practice self-care

If you don't believe you're an awesome person, you can forget to take care of yourself properly and focus on other people instead.

Five types of self-care to help get you started are:

Physical – Move your body. Go walking, dance to Sia. Make sure you are also sleeping properly and eating with a healthy diet in mind.

Social - If you have some friends, spend time with them. If not, make time for family who want the best for you.

Mental – Try to do things to keep your brain active. Anything from Wordle to doing a cool puzzle or reading a book you always wanted to; something that inspires or fascinates you.

Spiritual – Never underestimate the power of meditation. Whether you are 9 or 90 years old, clearing your mind daily is like weeding the flowerbeds. Practice whatever means a lot to you, and really focus on the moment.

Emotional – How do you process your emotions? Do you like to talk to your parents or siblings? Do you have a journal? Finding ways to express your feelings will lift the lid from time to time so that your emotions don't boil over.

Learn to accept compliments

OK, I know this one will bite, but even through gritted teeth, you have to start accepting compliments.

People aren't going to lie to you when they tell you something good about yourself. If someone wants to high-five you with words, smile and say thanks!

How to identify your strengths

It's hard to think about your strengths if all you are used to is talking negatively about yourself. Here are some ways you can find out what you're good at:

1. **Journal** – Write down good things about yourself and what you like doing and have achieved. Throw in items you can do well and enjoy doing too. Make that list as long as your arm and read it when you have negative thoughts about yourself. Journaling is such a cool way to spot patterns, especially when you look back at bad days and see the thoughts that crept up in response.

2. **Ask loved ones what they think you're best at** – They know you sometimes better than you know yourself. Loved ones will give you all the compliments all of the time if they can!

3. **Write down things you enjoy doing and why** – Great to reflect on when you are stuck for something to do or need a pick me up.

4. **Look for patterns** – Looking at patterns will help you see where you might be going wrong or how negativity starts in your life.

In this chapter, you have taken a huge look at your self-esteem and strengths. Lizzie worked hard to find the positives inside her, and she wants to share her experience with you.

Meet Lizzie, 20

Inspired by the following quote:

> *"I never had full awareness or answers about this condition. When I have more information, it actually helps me. It doesn't scare me once I know it."* – Selena Gomez

'I've always found it challenging to make friends. I used to play with imaginary friends when I was a little girl because I could always control what we played and how they felt about me. It felt nice to just be myself and play freely without fear of judgment, but as I got older, that changed.

I started school and was suddenly surrounded by all these other kids my age who knew how to make friends. It made me not feel good enough, and I thought all these crazy thoughts like everybody hated me and didn't want to hang out with me.

I was never invited to sleepovers, and those who I did talk to, I never let get too close to me because I didn't want to be rejected, so I kept everyone at arm's length.

Eventually, high school pushed me closer to a few girls, and we became friends, but I had to work really hard to think I was good enough to have them in my life.

I used to keep a journal because my older sister told me it might help me start to think about my negative thoughts, and it became clear that I was catastrophizing, always thinking about the worst-case scenario.

*My tip for anyone experiencing low self-esteem would be to start making <u>small changes</u> in how **you let** your voice talk to you.*

Turn the negativity into a super annoying person and start telling them to go away!'

Now, it's time to uncover <u>your</u> strengths!

Action step: practice self-care

What is the one thing you can do today that is an act of self-care? Don't overcomplicate it; just one simple thing that you can do. Go further and think of something you can do every day for the next week, keeping track of your progress as you go along.

Self-care today: _____

Self-care for the week: _____

Automatic thought	Cognitive distortions	Rational response

Action step: 5-minute triple-column technique

OK, so here's what you do. You can open Excel or Google Spreadsheet and create three columns.

First, write your 'automatic thought'
(Whatever the mean voice tells you). Ex. 'I have no friends. This sucks'.

Second, read it back, then look for those cognitive distortions.
Overthinking? Mental filter? What do you see? Whatever you notice goes in the second column. It could be just one thing, like overthinking or over-generalization. It could be more, though.

In the third column goes your 'rational response' – this is the logical part of your brain getting to work.
So it could be that you reword your automatic thought to read, 'I might not have many friends, but I can work to make some.'

This is a game-changer!

Action step: Keep a daily automatic thought log

Note any thought that keeps coming back and being a real pain. You can go back to this anytime in your day to see if you notice any patterns or matches with cognitive distortions.

Action step: Keep a replacement thought journal

Journaling is such a great, low-pressure way to explore negative thoughts. Try and aim for 2-3 times per week by writing unhelpful thoughts, then challenge them with the following questions:

- Where did this thought come from?
- When did I start thinking this way?
- Is this thought true?
- Is it helpful?
- Is it kind?
- Does it get me closer to being the person I want to be?
- What are some other ways to view the situations that are thoughtful and kind?

Reflection: What is the one thing you're proud of accomplishing this week?
You may want to jump right in and be negative or say nothing amazing happened, but truthfully, it doesn't need to be amazing. Reflect on anything that brought a little pride into your life, and don't dismiss it.

_____

_____

_____

_____

_____

_____

Action step: Keep a gratitude journal

Mornings or evenings work best, but it's about writing down **3 things you're grateful for and why.** When you feel negative, you can look back into this journal and review all the fantastic things you've got going for you that you wrote.

Action step: Thought stopping

When you have these crazy and intrusive thoughts, you can use this technique to stop them, replacing them with more positive ones instead.

In steps, you'll go through the following:

- Identify your unwanted thought or worry.

- Stop it! Literally, say it out loud or inside your mind. Clapping your hands or getting up and moving around is also effective.

- Replace the initial thought with a positive one.

You're diverting the negative energy away – and creating space for happier thoughts.

Action step: Develop a self-care plan

Tailored specially to suit you, it's always a great idea to develop your own bespoke self-care plan. Let's look at what that could involve:

Assess your needs:

Think about and write down what you consider to be major things you need to address. Less screen time, more sleep, or even thinking about joining a club at school to meet new people could all be on the list.

_____

_____

_____

_____

_____

_____

Consider your stressors:

When you are going about your day, what creates inner chaos? What things stress you out and make you retreat? When you know what your stressors are, you can work to shut them up.

_____

_____

_____

_____

_____

_____

Devise self-care strategies:

How can you intervene when things get really messy? Think about everything you've learned so far that can help you become the person you want to be and squash the anxiety and fear.

Ways to help with your anxiety can also be to go on a nice hike, or practice yoga, as these exercises bring us back to the moment.

- **Plan for challenges**

   When you know you have a big day approaching at school or socially, how can you plan for it? If you can prepare some thoughts or scenarios in your head, you can work out ways to squash them when they present themselves to you.

- **Take small steps**

   You have to jump in with both feet. Nothing happens overnight, but it's in the small changes that miracles can happen and, in turn, blow your mind.

- **Schedule time to focus on your needs**

   Make time for yourself. Ten minutes each day to start. Do something you love. Dance to your favorite song, thumb through your saved TikTok's, or whatever you want. Do something that makes you a priority.

Self-Assessment Quiz:

These questions vary with their scores. Some that point toward low self-esteem will give you a high mark, and others will offer you a lower mark.

I have purposely mixed them up randomly to make you think a *little* harder about yourself.

Give it a go!

0 = absolutely no way, earth swallow me up, I hate myself
5 = I feel on top of the world, want to dance the night away with *insert celeb crush here*

1.   Overall, I am happy with myself.

       0   1   2   3   4   5

2.   At times, I think I am no good at all.

       0   1   2   3   4   5

3.   I have some incredible qualities.

       0   1   2   3   4   5

4.   I can make friends easily.

       0   1   2   3   4   5

5.   I am never proud of myself.

      0   1   2   3   4   5

6.   I am a positive person.

      0   1   2   3   4   5

7.   I feel like a failure.

      0   1   2   3   4   5

8.   I wish I thought nicer things about myself.

      0   1   2   3   4   5

If you scored highly on questions 1, 2, 3, 4, and 6, you are working towards high self-esteem. If they were low scores, then you are experiencing low self-esteem.

If you scored highly for 5 and 7, those are considered negative towards your self-esteem, but the lower scores will give a more positive look into how you're feeling.

See if you can try these questions on different days and see how your scores change.

How do you feel?

This chapter has proven that you cannot only recognize where your negative talk comes from but also that you can silence it!

If you were ever in doubt of your abilities, now should be the time to correct that thought as you continue to ace the reading of this book and understand your anxiety.

It isn't easy making friends, but there is an incredible girl inside of you who deserves the love and care of at least one amazingly awesome friend.

Are you ready for more?

Chapter 3

How do I deal? Controlling your emotions.

We wouldn't be normal if we didn't have different emotions from one day to the next. Everybody experiences highs and lows, happiness and sadness, and so on.

Emotions come and go in waves, depending on what is currently going on in our lives, but when they become too strong to manage, understandably, they can freak us out.

In looking at the role emotions play in our lives, we can begin to see how the really strong and overwhelming ones can be controlled.

When you can face your emotions with more control, you can tackle the tricky ones and eventually get to a point where you are confident being in situations that offer you the chance to make *real friends*. You may not feel that's possible now, but it will be.

What are emotions?

We experience emotions every day, but so many girls can't quite put their finger on exactly how they feel if someone asks.

Essentially, emotions are reactions we experience in response to events or situations. How we feel is based on what is going on around us. The confusion begins when we respond differently to the same things!

That shouldn't invalidate your emotions, though. Emotions give us information, which is why even the tough ones are still super important to experience.

To wrap your head around it, let's look at the three key elements of emotions.

3 key elements of emotions:

1. Subjective experience – you are you, and I am me!

Let's be honest; if you get really nervous at the thought of a sleepover, but other girls get majorly excited at the same thought, you're looking at a subjective experience. We don't all feel the same or react in the same or even similar ways. It doesn't make you a freak! It makes you human.

2. Physiological response – Feeling it in the body.

If you have ever felt totally sick with anxiety or felt your heart palpitate, you'll know how connected your emotions are to your physiology. Remember the fight or flight response? It's exactly that.

3. Behavioral response – Express yourself!

Ah, yes, the sweet expression of emotion. It comes easy to so many, right? For others, it's so tricky to master showing how we feel because we just don't know how to.

Better yet, you spend your days thinking, 'Why did she react that way?' or 'Why can't I be that cool around other people?'

There are universal expressions, though, and one, in particular, that's always good to practice – smiling!

Emotions, feelings, and mood

Emotions change all the time, but we feel and experience each one with good reason – the cause!

If you have an argument with a friend, you'll likely experience anger. This anger might feel like frustration because your friend wasn't listening to what you were saying or they kept shutting you down. Their anger might feel like jealousy over the cause of the argument in the first place.

So, it's pretty easy to say you were both annoyed, but for different reasons based on those subjective experiences.

Moods don't last forever; they are just temporary emotional states. Sometimes you know why they have surfaced, while other times you might be like, huh?!

#confused!

How to deal with strong emotions

Counting to ten was *so* last year. Now there are helpful and practical ways to deal with the wave of emotion heading for your shores.

Let's look at two types of coping skills:

1) Problem-based

This coping skill is so helpful when you need to change what's causing your emotion. Like if you have this one friend who teases or criticizes you, your anxiety may be increased around her. A problem-based coping skill would be to end the friendship rather than put up with all that anxious junk she brings with her wherever she goes.

2) Emotion-based

When you don't want to or cannot change that situation, you will want to take care of your emotions. It's like, 'I cannot control this situation, so I have to learn ways to keep myself healthy as I go through it.'

Making time for yourself or even just being aware of your feelings can go a long way to help during those moments.

Don't think there aren't ways to help you in the moments you feel overwhelmed by emotion because there are so many!

Helpful thoughts for 'in the moment':

- I'm doing the best I can.
- I've been through this before and survived. I can do it again!
- Feeling like I can't cope doesn't mean I can't.
- This feeling won't last forever. It will eventually fade, and something better will come along.
- I can't change what's happening, so I will not focus on making it worse.

Helpful thoughts for any time:

- It's OK to feel angry or sad in some situations.

- We're all different and feel things differently.
- I've got people on my side who love me and want the best for me.
- Life is so confusing. I don't have to have all the answers today.
- It's important not to see things as black or white.

Helpful things to do:

- Take a shower or a bath.
- Call a loved one.
- Listen to some cool music.
- Catch a new video on YouTube.
- Do something nice for someone else.

Act opposite to an emotion's 'action urge'

When we experience different emotions, they try to permit us to act in specific ways.

For example, if you feel sad, you might not want to spend time with the people you care about. Or if you are caught up in anxiety, you might want to get away from what's causing it, like a presentation at school.

When you give power to the emotion, you can almost give them *permission* to crop back up any time and do it all over again. It is everything we feel we shouldn't do to face things that make us feel uncomfortable, but when we do, it can help us change the entire experience.

Distract yourself

This is *very* different from ignoring your emotions. While it is essential to recognize how you feel when you are put in a situation that you hate, you can find distractions around you.

Focusing on the blue sky or thinking about your favorite songs can help you just step back from the moment and find a little head space.

Use mindfulness

Mindfulness is a popular word, but there's a reason for that: it is very effective! Feeling your feet on the floor or the breeze in the air are both ways to immediately ground yourself and focus on the now...More about that to come!

Take some space from the situation

- **Take a walk** – Getting up and moving can get rid of the anxious energy you've got going on inside of you, and it is something many people do to try and release some of the emotions they are feeling.

- **Talk to a loved one** – People who know you well, genuinely care about you. You might think they don't sometimes, but they do! Make the most of this by reaching out when you need to. It can be as simple as just a catch-up or gossip about what's happening in the world.

- **Read or write** – Getting lost in the word of literacy is sooo therapeutic. Whether it's your thoughts, you're writing, or maybe even a book, do it!If you prefer to read, grab the book of your choice and snuggle down for a bit of escapism.

What is mindfulness? How can I use it to manage my emotions?

You read a snippet about mindfulness just now, but to break it down for you a little more:

Mindfulness is the ability to focus our attention on the present moment in a relaxed and non-judgmental fashion.

When we are mindful, we don't get caught up in worries about the future or what happened in the past. It's accepting that we can't predict or control what will happen and that we can't change what's been and gone.

So many people think this is such a weird concept. It takes practice to be able to nail it, but once you do, everything changes. The calm you feel will be totally worth the little bit of effort.

Let's look at 9 tips for practicing mindfulness to get you started.

9 Tips for practicing mindfulness:

1) Remember – it's cool if you don't feel relaxed

Mindfulness isn't about smelling the roses and being totally chill all the time. It isn't a relaxation exercise; it's an attention exercise. If you shift your attention from your anxiety to the present moment, that's a true diversion of energy.

2) Don't judge your thoughts

When you practice mindfulness, try not to judge the thoughts that come up. I mean, there is no such thing as a dumb thought. The trick is to let whatever thoughts you do have flow right out of you. Observe them, don't be them.

3) Find small moments to practice

You don't have to set aside hours a day to sit still and think about the present moment, could you imagine? You'd literally get nothing done. Instead, think about just walking and what you can see or hear. Even eating can be mindful - the taste of your food or the texture of what you're eating.

4) Have patience

This is a biggy, but it is important not to give up. Would you give up if you were learning a new TikTok dance? Likely not. So go ahead and treat this like you'd treat that and keep persisting with it. Eventually, it will all fall into place.

5) Don't seek control

You don't want to be able to control your thoughts – this is not the goal of mindfulness! It's human nature for our minds to wander, and the more we try not to think about something (oooh, ice cream sundaes), the more we think about it. Don't punish yourself. Just let the thought come and go like a cloud.

6) Be kind to yourself

Frustration will lead you to a muddy path of low self-esteem and self-judgment. Avoid! Just keep going and concentrate on your breathing and senses.

7) Don't believe everything you think

Could you imagine?! If we believed everything we thought, we'd be an absolute wrecking ball. You can have thoughts, but you don't have to believe them. Learn the difference and continue to work toward letting it come naturally.

8) Acceptance

Accepting what the present moment offers us is another big one because you are more likely to let it back out again. Don't hold onto a thought or feeling you don't like, even if you are experiencing it. Let it go, girl.

9) It all passes

It's like watching a twig float down a stream. Everything passes, and nothing is permanent. Everything comes and goes, and we simply sit nearby, watching it happen.

How to practice mindfulness meditation

There are great ways to help you meditate while practicing mindfulness. These steps are super helpful.

1. Try to remove all distractions from your room, like your phone. Sit or lie in a comfortable position.

2. Focus on your breathing. Inhale for 10 counts, then hold your breath for 10 counts. Exhale for 10 counts. Repeat five times.

3. Inhale and tense your body. Pause, relax, and exhale. Repeat five times.

4. Notice your breath and body. If a body part feels tight, consciously release it.

5. When a thought comes up, slowly return your focus to your breathing.

Strategies

**Here are some helpful strategies to practice mindfulness
when it comes to your emotions:**

- Emotions as waves – View your emotions as waves that come and go.
  Don't sit in your anxiety; release it back into the world.

- Now is not forever – If you feel overwhelmed, know that you have
  been here before and recovered. Feeling anxious and being anxious
  are two different things.

- Be accepting – If you think about emotions as a change in the
  weather, we can learn that it isn't always stormy in our skies!

- Be aware of your body – Feel what it is like to shake the tension out
  of your body. Label each sensation for what it is, and accept that it's
  how you're currently feeling rather than fighting it.

Inducing the relaxation response

If you find it difficult to calm down or get back to feeling relaxed, here are
some really cool ways to help you get there:

Meditation

Never underestimate the power of meditation! Seriously, it calms the body and mind and gets easier the more you do it. Different types of meditation are:

- **Mindfulness meditation** – The most popular type, focusing on the present moment.

- **Spiritual meditation** – This can be deep prayer or connecting to a higher power.

- **Focused meditation** – Using your five senses to focus your attention, like staring at a candle flame or counting your breaths.

- **Movement meditation** – This could be walking, tai chi, gardening, or anything that involves moving.

- **Mantra meditation** – Mantras are words, phrases, or sounds that you use, such as 'om.' Quietly or loudly, people like to focus on the sound.

- **Transcendental meditation** – Usually taught by a certified practitioner, it's designed to quiet the mind and induce a state of calm.

- **Progressive relaxation** – Most people use this as a body scan, starting from the top. Tensing and relaxing muscles to be aware of your body and imagining a gentle wave washing the tension away.

- **Loving-kindness meditation** – Sending loving messages out into the world and being open to receiving them through meditation, promoting love, compassion, and kindness.

- **Visualization meditation** – If you can create a negative narrative, you can create positive ones too! It is about vividly visualizing a scene and imagining you winning in life!

Start small – aim for like 5 or 10 minutes a day. Don't overwhelm yourself or add pressure to the moment.

Soon, you will be able to go longer, and it will become easier.

Breathing exercises

Here are 10 breathing exercises to help you find calm during really stressful times:

1. Pursed lip breathing

This breathing technique makes you slow down your breathing pace by getting you to breathe purposefully.

Try using this breath 4 to 5 times a day.

<u>To do it:</u>
1. Relax your neck and shoulders.
2. Keeping your mouth closed, inhale slowly through your nose for 2 counts.
3. Pucker or purse your lips as though you were going to whistle.
4. Exhale slowly by blowing air through your pursed lips for a count of 4.

2. Diaphragmatic breathing

Belly breathing can help you use your diaphragm properly.
Give diaphragmatic breathing a go for 5 to 10 minutes 3 to 4 times per day.
When you begin, you may feel tired, but it will ease over time.

<u>To do it:</u>
1. Lie on your back with your knees slightly bent and your head on a pillow.
2. You may place a pillow under your knees for support.
3. Place one hand on your upper chest and one below your rib cage, allowing you to feel the movement of your diaphragm.
4. Slowly inhale through your nose, feeling your stomach pressing into you hand.
5. Keep your other hand as still as possible.
6. Exhale using pursed lips as you tighten your stomach muscles, keeping your upper hand completely still

3. Breath focus technique

This deep breathing technique uses imagery or focus words and phrases.
You can choose a focus word that makes you smile or feel relaxed. Examples include peace, let go, or relax, but it can be any word that works for you.
You can start with a 10-minute session and go up from there.

To do it:

1. Sit or lie down in a comfortable place.
2. Bring your awareness to your breaths without trying to change how you're breathing.
3. Alternate between regular and deep breaths a few times.
4. Notice how shallow breathing feels compared to deep breathing.
5. Practice your deep breathing for a few minutes.
6. Place one hand below your belly button, keeping your belly relaxed, and notice how it rises with each inhale and falls with each exhale.
7. Let out a loud sigh with each exhale.
8. Begin the practice of breath focus by combining this deep breathing with imagery and a focus word or phrase that will support relaxation.
9. You can imagine that the air you inhale brings waves of peace and calm throughout your body. Mentally say, "Inhaling peace and calm."
10. Imagine that the air you exhale washes away tension and anxiety. You can say to yourself, "Exhaling tension and anxiety."

4. Lion's breath

Lion's breath is an exercise frequently used in yoga.

To do this:

1. Come into a comfortable seated position. You can sit back on your heels or cross your legs.
2. Press your palms against your knees with your fingers spread wide.
3. Inhale deeply through your nose and open your eyes wide.
4. At the same time, open your mouth wide and stick out your tongue, bringing the tip down toward your chin.
5. Contract the muscles at the front of your throat as you exhale out through your mouth by making a long "ha" sound.

6. You can turn your gaze to look at the space between your eyebrows or the tip of your nose.
7. Do this breath 2 to 3 times.

5. Alternate nostril breathing

Alternate nostril breathing is a breathing practice for relaxation.
Alternate nostril breathing has been shown to enhance cardiovascular function and lower heart rate. Avoid this if you're feeling sick or congested. Keep your breath smooth and even throughout the practice.

To do this:
1. Choose a comfortable seated position.
2. Lift your right hand toward your nose, pressing your first and middle fingers down toward your palm and leaving your other fingers extended.
3. After an exhale, gently use your right thumb to close your right nostril.
4. Inhale through your left nostril and then close your left nostril with your right pinky and ring fingers.
5. Release your thumb and exhale out through your right nostril.
6. Inhale through your right nostril and then close this nostril.
7. Release your fingers to open your left nostril and exhale through this side.
8. This is one cycle.
9. Continue this breathing pattern for up to 5 minutes.
10. Finish your session with an exhale on the left side.

6. Equal breathing

The equal breathing technique focuses on making your inhales and exhales the same length. Making your breath smooth and steady can help bring about balance in the moment.

You should find a breath length that is not too easy or too difficult. You also don't want it to be too fast so that you're able to maintain it throughout. Usually, this is between 3 and 5 counts.

To do this:
1. Choose a comfortable seated position.
2. Breathe in and out through your nose.
3. Count during each inhale and exhale to ensure they are even in duration. Alternatively, choose a word or short phrase to repeat during each inhale and exhale.
4. You can add a slight pause or breath retention after each inhale and exhale if you feel comfortable. (Normal breathing involves a natural pause.)
5. Continue practicing this breath for at least 5 minutes.

7. Resonant or coherent breathing

Resonant breathing, also known as coherent breathing, is when you breathe at a rate of 5 full breaths per minute. You can achieve this rate by inhaling and exhaling for a count of 5. Breathing at this rate reduces so much stress!

To do this:
1. Inhale for a count of 5.
2. Exhale for a count of 5.
3. Continue this breathing pattern for at least a few minutes.

8. Sitali breath

This yoga breathing practice helps you lower your body temperature and relax your mind.

Slightly extend your breath in length but don't force it. Since you inhale through your mouth, choose a place to practice that's free of dust and allergies.

To do this:
1. Choose a comfortable seated position.
2. Stick out your tongue and curl your tongue to bring the outer edges together.
3. If your tongue doesn't do this, you can purse your lips.
4. Inhale through your mouth.
5. Exhale out through your nose.
6. Continue breathing like this for up to 5 minutes.

9. Deep breathing

Deep breathing helps relieve shortness of breath by preventing air from getting trapped in your lungs and allowing you to breathe in more fresh air. It may help you to feel more relaxed and centered.

To do this:
1. While standing or sitting, draw your elbows back slightly to allow your chest to expand.
2. Take a deep inhalation through your nose.
3. Retain your breath for a count of 5.
4. Slowly release your breath by exhaling through your nose.

10. Humming bee breath

Some people use humming bee breath to relieve frustration, anxiety, and anger. This breathing practice's unique sensation helps create instant calm and is incredibly soothing around your forehead. Of course, you'll want to practice it where you won't look odd making a humming sound!

To do this:
1. Choose a comfortable seated position.
2. Close your eyes and relax your face.
3. Place your first fingers on the tragus cartilage that partially covers your ear canal.
4. Inhale and gently press your fingers into the cartilage as you exhale.
5. Keeping your mouth closed, make a loud humming sound.
6. Continue for as long as is comfortable.

Progressive muscle relaxation

Progressive muscle relaxation (PMR) is basically tensing and relaxing your muscles until you become aware of the difference so that you are more likely to know when you are feeling uptight. It was first introduced by an American physician called Edmund Jacobson in the 1930s.

When you experience anxiety, you probably know the tense feeling I'm talking about! If you practice PMR, you'll learn how a relaxed muscle feels different from a tense muscle.

Meet Annie, 18

Inspired by the following quote:

'It's amazing what you can get if you quietly, clearly,
and authoritatively demand it'
- Meryl Streep

'My mom has always meditated, and I used to laugh at her because it was strange seeing her totally zone out of life. Looking back, I think it was just a mixture of curiosity and envy because I wanted to try it and feel the reward of relaxing.

I started to do it before school to help me get in the zone. It was good practice for when I got there, and things felt overwhelming because I started to know how to handle those feelings better.

Fast forward four years, and
I'm still going every day!

I don't regret starting at all,
and my advice to girls in the
same boat as I was, is just to
try it and start small. You'll
literally never go back.'

Meet Mel, 20

Inspired by the following quote:

> 'Our life is shaped by our mind, for we think what we become.'
> – Buddha

'My neighbor had this quote on a plaque in her garden, and I always remembered reading it as a kid. I never appreciated what it meant until I had to move and start a new school. I was totally freaked out, wondering if everyone would just disown me.

I didn't want the attention that came with being the new girl, but I remembered the quote the night before that first day.

I Googled mindfulness as I'd heard the word but didn't really understand what it meant, and I ended up just sitting on the floor of my new bedroom breathing.

At first, it was weird; I felt like I should be doing something more, but after ten minutes, I felt so calm. I was still nervous about going to school, but I promised myself I would try to get familiar with that relaxing feeling, so I carried on every day on my bedroom floor, eventually doing it in my garden when the weather was nice!

My tip for other girls would be not to be afraid to try something new.'

Ready to give it a go?

How to do progressive muscle relaxation

As the PMR mentioned before, the girls' stories will be the first thing you can start to get involved with.

- First, find a quiet place with no distractions.
- Lie on the floor or recline in a chair, where ever you feel most comfortable.
- Loosen any tight clothing, and remove your glasses or contacts if you wear them.
- Rest your hands in your lap or wherever is comfortable.
- Take a few slow and even breaths.
- Now, turn your focus to the following areas, but try and leave the rest of your body relaxed:

- Forehead: Squeeze and release the muscles every 15 seconds. Feel them get tight and feel them relax.
- Jaw: Tense for 15 seconds and release for 30.
- Neck and shoulders: Increase the tension here by raising your shoulders toward your ears and holding for 15 seconds. Release for 30.
- Arms and hands: Slowly draw both hands into a fist, pull them toward your chest and hold for 15 seconds. Slowly release for 30.
- Buttocks: Slowly increase the tension for 15 seconds, and release for 30.
- Legs: Slowly increase the tension in your quads and calves over 15 seconds. Gently release for 30.
- Feet: Slowly increase the tension in your feet and toes as much as you can for 15 seconds, then release for 30.

You will feel so relaxed once you work from head to toe!

Action step: identify your emotions

The next time you experience a strong emotion, ask yourself:

- What am I feeling right now?

_____

_____

_____

- What happened to make me feel this way?

_____

_____

_____

- Does this situation have a different explanation that might make sense?

_____

_____

_____

- What do I want to do about these feelings?

_____

_____

_____

- Is there a better way of coping with them?

_____

_____

_____

Action step: Keep a mood journal

Mood journals are great for getting to the root of your problems and helping increase positive ones. It's about recording your feelings rather than what you did in your day.

You can create columns in your journal, something along these lines (with an example given included):

Emotion Name.	What caused this emotion?	Behaviors or actions this emotion caused me to make.	Is this emotion helpful to the situation?	Is this situation horrible to put up with, or a problem to solve? And how?
Anxiety	Needing to do a science presentation at school	I sweat; I asked to use the bathroom, where I freaked out and cried.	Nope...	It's horrible, but I need to do it, so I should try and be mindful and get through it with the help of notes. Everyone has to do it.

Do you see how easy it is to reflect on uncomfortable situations?
Please give it a shot yourself!

How do you feel?

We've given you a full body scan to check your mental and physical well-being! Are you ready to dive into the practical side of making friends?

The first step in making a new friend can be completely overwhelming:

In the next chapter, we will look at how to turn this vomit-inducing activity into something enjoyable!

Chapter 4

Wanna chat? The secret to good conversations.

Having a conversation with someone else can be enough to leave you completely freaked out, wanting to lock yourself in your room for days.

You might think conversations are awkward, uncomfortable, strange, or just plain NO.

There is so much more to holding a good conversation than just saying whatever comes to your mind (which can be fatal!)

How can you learn to do it your own way?

The basics of a good conversation

There are ways to have good and meaningful conversations with people, but the secret is knowing how to get started without freaking out and avoiding the situation altogether.

Active listening

Active listening is when you want to hear more than just the words somebody is speaking to get more out of how they say those words and their intent. Meaning the other person feels totally heard and respected.

12 Awesome tips - Starting conversations with people you don't know

- **Get involved** – sports, clubs, volunteering, community service.

- **Smile!!** – the easiest, most effective tool that everyone can do!

- **Talk to people** - ask questions about them. People love to talk about themselves.

- **Have some stories** - share recent experiences, struggles, or challenges.

- **Offer help** - make sure it's give and take.

- **Share** – this is a great convo starter – food (yum! Everyone loves some gum or snacks), notes, pens, or paper.

- **Relax** – use some of the breathing exercises discussed previously (Woo-saahhh).

- **Friend people you meet** – find them on social.

- **Invite them to do things** - something you like.

- **Accept invitations** - once you have some rapport, then you can pick and choose.

- **Stay in touch** - shows you care and are a good friend.

- **Give compliments** – How amazing is your day when someone says something nice about you? People love compliments!

As frightening as it sounds, you can start a conversation with so many different people. Many of you may find it difficult and particularly stressful if you suffer from anxiety. Still, improving your social skills and becoming more comfortable chatting with people is possible.

Let's take a look:

Strategies

- **Start with baby steps**
  Strike up a conversation with the barista at Starbucks or the cashier at the grocery store. You know you'll be gone in a few minutes, which can help you overcome the initial discomfort.

- **Comment on something personal**
  Whether it's a unique piece of jewelry or an unusual shirt you like, let them know how cool it is!
  - 'Wow, that is such a cool necklace!'
  - 'Nice shirt! So you like Billie Eilish?'

- **Ask if you've met before**
  This can be cool at the right moment. 'You seem familiar; do I know you from somewhere?' can lead to talking about whether or not you go to the same school or if you may have passed each other in a coffee shop or library somewhere.

- **Use humor in a positive way**
  Humor is a great way to bond with someone. You might be in a new class, sitting next to them. You could say, 'Doesn't that guy over there look like Harry Potter?' Try not to be mean or judgmental but keep it light and fun. You may meet your humor twin!

- **Keep the conversation going**

  Just because you may be anxious, or have an anxiety diagnosis, doesn't mean you can't keep up your end of the conversation, even though it can be challenging.

- **Practice your communication skills with trusted loved ones**

  It's a great way to build your confidence and test what may or may not work in real-life scenarios. You may get some advice back too!

- **Remember that you're not a mind reader**

  You may think the other person is having a dreadful time talking to you, but you don't know that for sure. Also, you don't know unless you ask! The art of conversation should *allow* your curiosity to find out more about them.

- **Let people know you'll be brief**

  This is so handy when you want to be short but sweet to grab people's attention.

- 'I am just about to head for lunch, but your gorgeous purse caught my eye.'
- 'I'm heading home, but I was wondering if you have plans this weekend...'

55 Questions to get to know someone

1. What's your favorite time of year?
2. What do you like to eat?
3. Do you play any sports?
4. What's your drink of choice?
5. Do you ever binge any TV shows?
6. Do you have a TikTok?
7. What's your favorite filter?
8. What hobby have you always wanted to do?
9. iPhone or Android?
10. What's your favorite candy?
11. Are you into collecting?
12. What's your favorite make-up brand?
13. Do you like to work out?
14. What's your star sign?
15. Do you watch YouTube?
16. What did you like as a kid?
17. What's your favorite band?
18. What would you do with a million dollars?
19. Do you like school?
20. What's your favorite ice cream?
21. Do you like Halloween?
22. What do you want to do when you leave school?
23. Who do you follow on social media?
24. Do you keep a diary?
25. Do you like dancing?
26. What shampoo do you use?
27. What do you do on the weekends?
28. Do you have pets?
29. Do you like school?
30. What's your favorite class?
31. Celeb crush?
32. What's the worst movie you've seen?
33. Favorite movie?
34. Home Alone 1 or 2?
35. What's your dream festival lineup?
36. Sunrise or sunset?
37. Are you a morning bird or a night owl?
38. Do you do yoga?
39. Where do you shop?
40. Do you have Netflix?
41. Favorite Disney movie?
42. Do you like Harry Potter?
43. Which Harry Potter house would you be in?
44. What's a huge movie you've never seen?
45. Best vacation ever?
46. Do you have a boyfriend/girlfriend?
47. Are your parents cool?
48. Do you like eating out?
49. If you could learn a language, which one would you pick?
50. Do you game?
51. Pumpkin spiced latte – yes or no?
52. Do you prefer Christmas or Thanksgiving?
53. What did you do during the lockdowns?
54. Do you believe in ghosts?
55. What scares you the most?

The 3 A's of active listening

The 3 A's are great for getting you started in any conversation.

Attention - Being fully tuned into what the other person is saying or how they are gesturing.

Attitude – Being positive and open-minded.

Adjustment – You can change how you come across to the listener with your body language, reactions to their words, and gestures.

How to practice active listening

1. **Pay attention**

   As much as 65% of a person's communication is unspoken. Paying attention to the way someone acts when they talk is really important. For example, if they are talking at a super-fast speed, it might be that they, too, are anxious, just like you. Speaking too slowly can mean they might be tired or carefully choosing their words.

2. **Reflect on what you hear**

   Once the other person has said what they want to say, tell them what you heard. You can ask further questions about the conversation, or you could paraphrase, like, 'In other words, what you're saying is you're frustrated,' or something like that.

3. **Withhold judgment**

   Letting people share their thoughts or feelings without shaming, blaming, or criticizing makes them feel they are being listened to and understood.

4. Ask open-ended questions

This is a great way to allow the natural flow of a conversation. Something as simple as, 'So how was your weekend?' means they can't reply with yes or no. You're creating a meaningful exchange.

5. Be patient

Remember that you may not be the only nervous one in the conversation, so be patient with the other person and with yourself. Don't cut yourself up over what you think are mistakes. Try your best.

Examples of active listening

Here are some examples of what active listening looks like:

> **Sarah***: I'm so sorry to dump this on you, but I had a fight with my sister, and we haven't spoken since. I don't know who to talk to. It's made me so upset.*

> **Jodie***: That's OK! Tell me more about what happened.* (Open-ended question)

> **Sarah***: We just got into a fight about what to do for our parent's anniversary. We couldn't agree on anything.*

> **Jodie***: Oh, that sounds tough. You sound really upset that you're still not speaking since it happened.* (Reflecting on what was heard)

> **Sarah***: Yes! OMG, she makes me so mad. She assumed I had the time to help her with this really fancy party – I have so much schoolwork to do! She refused to listen to me.*

Jodie: *That sounds so awful. How do you feel about it?*
(another open-ended question)

Sarah: *PO'd. Frustrated. Invisible. I guess guilty, too, as I have so much going on right now, and I was the one saying no. I just told her to plan it all without me, but I know that isn't right, either.*

Jodie: *Sounds like you're processing it all! I bet you need a little time to sort out how you feel now.* (Withholding judgment)

Sarah: *I think I do. Thanks for listening, girl. I appreciate you letting me vent.*

Benefits of active listening

In listening this way, you can start to:

- See positive improvements at school.
- Begin to find it easier to talk to people and eventually make a few friends.
- It can also be a major confidence boost!
- Avoid conflict.

Assertive communication

You can be clear about what you want to say and get your thoughts, feelings, and opinions out there without putting theirs down.

Remember that it can be **HARD**:

- **H**onest
- **A**ppropriate
- **R**espectful
- **D**irect

It does, however, get easier to do with time.

Types of communication

Let's take a look at the following types of communication:

Assertive
Being honest but kind in a respectful way.

Aggressive
This is a harsh, demanding, or hostile manner to speak to someone and should be avoided.

Passive-aggressive
You know when someone says something mean but with a really kind tone of voice? That is to be passive-aggressive. It doesn't make it right, but sulking, ignoring the other person, or acting innocent when you complain or criticize can all mean you or they are being like this.

5 steps to effective, assertive communication

You can learn to strengthen your own communication with these 5 steps:

- **Be clear with what you don't like**
  If you don't like how someone is being, stick to the facts rather than label them or use judgy comments.

  Don't say, for example, *'Oh my God, you're so rude! You're always late!'*, and instead try, *'We were supposed to meet at 11:30, but now it is 11:50.'*

- **Don't judge or exaggerate**
  Don't go all dramatic on people or what they say.
  'Now lunch is completely ruined!' can be replaced with, *'I have less time to spend at lunch now because class starts at 1.'*

- **Use 'I' messages**
  Spend way less time starting sentences with 'You' and try more starting with 'I.' *'I'd like it if you stopped that,'* sounds much better than, *'You need to stop that!'*

- **Put it all together!**
  'When you *(talking about them)*, I feel *(your feelings are expressed here)*.'
  For example, *'When you yell, I feel attacked.'*

- **List behavior, results, and feelings**
  To be more detailed than the point prior:
  When you (their behavior), then (the results of their behavior), and I feel (how you feel).
  For example, *'When you ignore me, I think I have done something wrong, and that makes me feel sad.'*

Body language

Using physical behavior, expressions, and mannerisms to communicate non-verbally is known as body language.

This can be a good thing – or a bad thing! Sometimes people can be so confused with what is being displayed by the other person that it can create moments of worry if you don't like what you see.

What is non-verbal communication?

Non-verbal communication is how we present ourselves without the art of talking.

These include:

- **Facial expressions**
  Surprise, happiness, anger, fear, sadness, and disgust can all show through facial expressions, which other people can read clearly.

- **Body movement and posture**
  Whether you're sitting, walking, hunching over, striding, or hovering over someone, it will tell others a lot about your current vibe.

- **Gestures**
  Gestures include waving, pointing, and even using hands when talking. Some people use these to really animate what they are saying.

- **Eye contact**
  It's crucial to look interested in the conversation; maintaining good eye contact is a great way to display this.

The pandemic kinda gave us a year or so off being able to have face-to-face conversations, but we are slowly getting there and making it work!

You can tell a lot by a person's eyes. Honesty, warmth, affection, and attraction can all come through, so use them well.

5 Roles of non-verbal communication:

- **Repetition**
  Repeat and strengthen the message you are speaking, literally.

- **Contradiction**
  Refrain from contradicting the message you're sending out by giving off different non-verbal vibes.

- **Substitution**
  You can substitute your verbal message with a simple facial expression.

- **Complementing**
  You might complement your verbal message with a nice gesture, like a fist bump!

- **Accenting**
  You can underline a verbal message like if you pound a table, it might underline the importance of what you're saying.

How non-verbal communication can go wrong

Like anything, non-verbal communication can go drastically wrong!
Two examples are:

1. *Lucy wanted to find out who was coming to her sleepover, so she asked two friends, who both said yes. Stacey was also invited and standing nearby over listening, but Lucy didn't ask her.*

    Stacey thought she was uninvited as Lucy didn't ask her. Stacey smiled at Lucy, who still didn't notice, and walked past her in the busy hall.

    Stacey got upset and thought nobody liked her.

    Was a missed smile enough for Stacey to think she was no longer invited? Definitely not!

2. *Jen forgot her glasses.*

    On the way to school, her somewhat shy friend waved to her from along the street. Jen saw a person moving frantically ahead of her but didn't assume it was aimed at her.

    She got on the bus and went to school, not knowing she had unintentionally ignored a good friend.

    Waving and not verbalizing to your friends can simply mean they don't see you, for good reason, in this case.

How to improve non-verbal communication and read body language

Here are some great and effective ways to get you started:

- **Stand tall**
  With your shoulders back and your arms unfolded, you can offer a warm, trustworthy, and confident welcome to those around you. Seeing someone slouched or hunched over can put off the vibe that you're not interested, tired, and generally unapproachable.

- **Avoid touching your face**
  This is especially good to avoid if you are being asked questions because it comes across as you being dishonest. It might not always be the case but try to avoid fiddling with your hair or scratching your nose just to be sure.

- **Smile more**
  Warm, sincere smiles are attractive, reassuring – and infectious!

- **Look interested**
  Imagine being spoken to and the other person looking like they couldn't care less. Always appear as if you are happy to be engaging in conversation, and you'll be more likely to have another opportunity to do so again!

- **Relax your body**
  Tension is not a great thing to feel in the body, but also, it shows other people when you're uptight, and they could think something is wrong.

Maintaining conversations

So, you've done it – you've struck up a cool conversation with a potential friend!

NOW WHAT?!

You have to keep it flowing, girl!

Here are some great ways to maintain a conversation:

- **Ask open-ended questions**
  Rather than going in with yes or no questions that shut down a conversation, such as:
  - Was school good yesterday?
  - Do you have an Instagram?

You can try these:

  - What did you do over the weekend?
  - What are your favorite memes right now?
  - How many brothers and sisters do you have?

- **Asking small talk follow-up questions**
  This shows you care about conversations and getting them past the chit-chat phase:

  You: *'What have you been up to today?'*
  Them: *'School, mainly.'*
  You: (follow up)*: 'How's your homework been lately?'*
  Them: *Well, I...'* (There is more motivation to progress the conversation and keep it flowing).

It can be stressful not knowing what to say when it comes to small talk, but it does get easier with time! Remember these TALK tips:

T – Time – be kind to yourself. Nothing happens overnight.
A – Appreciation – Appreciate just being in the moment and add in something funny or cool you might spot during your talk that could cover up an awkward silence.
L – Laugh – If something is funny, go ahead and laugh. It's catchy!
K – Kindness – If you show you care about the conversation, you will likely have another.

Balance between sharing and asking questions to get to know someone.

Conversations need to be balanced to be successful. The IFR method works really well:

- Inquire – Ask a sincere question (*What's your ideal weekend?*)
- Follow – Ask a follow-up question (*Oh cool, so you like to sleep in?*)
- Relate – Share something about you to break up your questions to balance the conversation (*I love staying up late and having lazy mornings!*)

Avoid asking too many questions

Appreciate that a conversation can sound more like a job interview with too many questions, so try to keep it light and share relevant things about yourself along the way. Conversations can go off on a tangent, and that's OK!

Be genuinely interested

When you ask questions to fill in uncomfortable silences, they sometimes come off as less sincere. Always show genuine interest in people when speaking to them.

Find mutual interests

When you want to jump the hurdle of small talk, you need to find a mutual interest to chat about. Asking questions about their interests or what they like can lead you to say, 'me too!' - and off you go!

Mutual interests not only make for good conversation, but they bond us. That's how we make and keep friends.

Practice being OK with silence at times

Silence is a natural part of conversations, but it's only awkward if you freak out and panic, making it so.

When you feel that pause mid-conversation, think that the other person is probably feeling it too, and it is just as likely up to them to initiate a new topic.

Play it cool and go with the flow. The other person will pick up on your relaxed vibe and feel the same comfort in those silences.

Return to a previous topic

When you hit a dead-end, you can go back in time and bring something the other person said to the present moment!

For example:

- 'So tell me about the trip to New York with your parents you mentioned earlier. I bet it was amazing.'
- 'Did you say before that you're reading a new series of books? What are they about?'

Tell a story

You can bring any conversation to life with a little tale! It's always cool to have two or three stories ready to bring up that can show you as a good person or a relatable friend.

Think about something funny you did or a really nice outcome to a recent situation. You may have something up your sleeve that could make someone laugh!

Ask for advice or a recommendation

Asking for advice about a topic they love is a great way to start a conversation about their interests. It'll also work out because you'll get some helpful information back!

Something like, 'Oh hey, your nails always look so good. I need a really good new gel nail polish. Which are your faves?' If you wanted to create a cool TikTok but have trouble editing, you could ask how they do theirs – the list is endless!

Stay positive

Avoid criticism, which is a conversation killer, and focus on the more positive ways to keep a conversation flowing.

Try challenging yourself to discover why someone likes their hobby or a fashion brand so much. You might be surprised by their answer!

If someone asks you a question, the chances are they'd be happy to talk about the same topic.

They might ask you what you like to do on the weekends, and you can happily list everything you love. Then that same question can be fired back, and boom! You have yourself a conversation.

Ending conversations

Sometimes you want to end a conversation without appearing rude, but it doesn't need to be complicated.

Just wrap things up without explanation

It's OK sometimes to say you have to go without an explanation, especially if you already know the person. They will totally understand!

- *'I gotta run; great talking to you!'*
- *'OK, cool, anyway I need to go, so I'll catch you another time.'*

These are both great examples.

The 'Anyway, I'll let you get back to it' classic

This is good for catching a quick chat with someone who was already in the middle of doing something.

- *'Anyway, it was good seeing you; I'll let you get back to your shopping.'*

Use a reason why you have to leave the conversation

This is good for excusing yourself if you feel overwhelmed or if you simply need to be somewhere else.

- *'It was so good seeing you; I need to get to dance class.'*
- *'Let's talk more at lunch, so we aren't late for the bus.'*
- *'I have to head to the bathroom; maybe I'll run into you later.'*

Use body language to show you're ready to leave the conversation

You can be friendly and polite while maintaining a shift in your body language. It lets people know you're ready to move on to something else.

- *Stand up if you have been sitting down.*
- *Start to move slowly toward the door.*
- *Look frequently in the direction you need to be heading.*

Summarize and wrap up the conversation

It's an excellent way to get to the conversation's end by summing it up.

- *'The movie sounds awesome; I can't wait! Anyway, I really should get going.'*
- *'I'm definitely going to give my profile that update when I get home. I'll let you know how I like the new filters.'*

Get back to your music/book/phone

Saying, 'I'm going to get back to my book now,' or, 'I am going to listen to my music,' are good ways of letting the other person know your intentions without being rude.

Reference future plans

Saying you have to be at a certain place at a specific time is a good way of ensuring you can leave the conversation promptly.

- *'I have to go in a few minutes, but I wanted to say hey real quick.'*

Say something kind (but genuine!)

'It's been so nice talking to you! Maybe we can do it again sometime?' is a great example of ending the conversation but letting the other person know you would love to catch up again soon.

Digital communication

It's tricky to get the tone right when communicating digitally. You also might freak out if someone doesn't reply right away.

Let's look a little deeper at digital communication tips.

Basic texting etiquette:

- **Remember that people have different texting styles**
  Don't take how they write personally! We're all different.

- **Use humor carefully**
  Ensure you aren't offending or reading too much into texts.

- **Use emojis!**
  Emojis are fun! Use them to express yourself.

- **Don't worry if someone doesn't answer right away**
  People can get busy, and that's cool. Be patient.

- **Use exclamation points or no punctuation**
  Learn how to be clear with your messages and the enunciation behind them.

Give friendly, meaningful answers in your texts; it's the perfect tool for digital communication, where you can still show active listening by responding and rephrasing.

Social media etiquette:

Keeping yourself safe online and ensuring you are not left vulnerable is so important.

How can you be safe and secure online? Let's take a look.

- **Everything is public**
  I mean everything! Even posts you have deleted; it's all traceable, so use your powers wisely.

- **Don't post while angry or upset**
  You'll regret sharing angry posts and letting others know about your business. They may form an opinion of you that isn't accurate.

- **Don't use all caps when emailing, posting, or texting**
  Using all caps can MAKE IT SEEM AS THOUGH YOU ARE SHOUTING!

- **Use different usernames and passwords for your sites**
  You don't want people figuring out your password for everything, so for maximum protection, shake things up.

- **Don't compare yourself to others**
  Nobody's life is perfect, so don't look at their highlights online and assume they have it way better; they don't. Anybody can be who they want online, so don't compare yourself to a standard that's so unrealistic.

- **Don't post pictures or videos of people without their permission.**
  A big one, but important. There are so many laws now, so be careful.

- **Don't take or send inappropriate pictures**
  Another biggy – you can't trust where that content will end up and who will see it. Take care of yourself and your body.

- **Remember not to be hurtful**
  They may be just words, but they can still cut like a knife. Be kind.

- **Be careful with personal information**
  Giving out your name, address, date of birth, card numbers, or phone number online is a no-no. This is confidential information for you only.

- **Minimize talking to strangers**
  At the end of the day, you don't know who they are, so talking to strangers should be kept to a minimum.

- **Remember that you're worth more than likes or comments**
  These might feel like they mean something to you, but you're worth more than likes or comments. You don't need external validation.

Advice - how to meet new people!

Beth, 19
'Just go to events you like, and see who else is there.'

Alexandra, 21
'Get out there and do stuff!'

Naomi, 20
'Hit them with a joke, it's a huge ice-breaker.'

Lexi, 21
'Smile and ask how their day is going.'

Rachel, 19
'Walk up to people and say hi and ask them their name.'

Kym, 18
'Be kind - people just like to be listened to.'

Time to chat!

Communication self-assessment

Here is a compiled set of questions to help you assess your current communication skills. Mark yourself 0 for not at all and 5 for yes, all the time!

- It's not OK to interrupt others
    0   1   2   3   4   5

- I make eye contact when I am speaking to someone else
    0   1   2   3   4   5

- I can make conversation with anybody
    0   1   2   3   4   5

- I have meaningful conversations often
    0   1   2   3   4   5

- I chat with anybody, even in a queue!
    0   1   2   3   4   5

- I find it easy to think of what to say next
    0   1   2   3   4   5

- I am genuinely interested in what people have to say
    0   1   2   3   4   5

- I pay lots of attention to body language
    0   1   2   3   4   5

- I am good at giving class presentations
  - 0 1 2 3 4 5

- I consider myself an active listener
  - 0 1 2 3 4 5

The higher the score, the more likely it is that you currently possess the right communication skills. But don't worry, if you scored lower– with a bit of time and effort, you could do anything!

Action step: Your turn!

How about trying to start one conversation this week? It could be a person at school, on the bus, or in line at the store.

Afterward, reflect on how it went. What felt easy? What was more difficult? How could you improve next time?

_____

_____

_____

How do you feel?

It's incredible what a simple look or gesture can do for yourself or someone else, right? Once you've learned how to communicate effectively, you can form super-strong friendships that last.

Next, we look at what these types of friendships look and feel like in real life.

Chapter 5

Are you my people? Finding the right friends.

With everything you've read so far, what do you think makes a good friend?

(Fill out this spider diagram!)

This chapter will offer you information and tips on finding good friends, keeping them, and maintaining healthy relationships for the long haul.

As human beings, we are *so* social, both online and off. We need to connect, but knowing how to start or who we should connect with can take time and effort.

So, let's dive in!

It can be done!

What makes a good friend?

It's a well-researched fact that the better the quality of your friendship, the more likely you are to be happy. In fact, it goes way further than simply 'being happy' - it improves your physical and mental health, making you less likely to suffer in the long run.

And hey – having good friends also makes you *live longer!*

Having great social connections in your life and developing and nurturing lasting friendships is essential.

Traits of a good friend:

1. Someone who listens

As we know, good listeners make good friends. When we listen and share, we build strong bonds. You can also learn a lot when you listen to others' points of view. Is it more important to have a friend who dismisses what you say or takes a genuine interest?

2. They don't judge you

Being accepted for who you are is the key to a good friendship. When we are often criticized or shamed for our opinions, it can lead to more anxiety and lower self-esteem.

3. They are kind and respectful

Good friends include you in events, so you don't feel left out. They respect your beliefs - be they cultural or social, and offer friendly gestures like time together, remembering birthdays, offering compliments, or simply asking you out for coffee. Be around kindness and deliver it back.

4. Someone loyal

When times get tough, the best thing about having a true friend is knowing you have someone on your side, someone there for you. Loyal friends are hard to come by, but once you find one, they will be there for life. It is truly the best gift to have.

5. Someone who laughs with you

You always, always, want someone to laugh with. Those memories you create with laughter will be forever remembered and referred to. 'Remember that time...?!'
When life throws us those curveballs, sharing laughs and funny stories really makes a difference – for the better!

6. They make you smile

Just being around them makes you feel happy. Good friends bring out the sunshine, even on the cloudiest of days. It can be seeing them in class or the lunch line – it's reassuring.

7. A strong friend who is self-confident

Here's a little fact about self-confidence: it is contagious! I'm not talking about the loud and intrusive type of confidence; I mean when we are in the company of people who are confident within themselves. This is the magical moment we can feel our confidence rise, which is beautiful.

8. A good friend shows empathy

When some things go wrong, as they always do, we look for people to understand us. In those times of need, a shoulder is good to cry on, but a level of 'that must be really tough for you' goes a long way.

How to make good friends

When the time comes, and you have an opportunity to make a good friend, you'll want to be armed with some tools up your sleeve so the moment doesn't pass you by in a blaze of sheer panic.

Let's look at some of these strategies to help get you started.

- **Put yourself out there**

Even if you aren't sure, take a step out of your comfort zone and try to put yourself in situations where someone will talk to you. Try a *different* table at lunch, sit in a different seat on the bus, or walk a different route to school. You could end up meeting someone who becomes an insta BFF.

- **Help other people**

Volunteering can be a great way to make new friends. It goes beyond helping at a local center or store; it can mean lending a hand in school. Is there a drama club? Maybe there is a need for props or a hair and make-up specialist.

Giving up your time to do something you don't usually do puts you in a place where you are _definitely_ going to meet new people.

It's worth checking out somewhere local for you to volunteer. Is there a cool record store you like to hang out at? Maybe your school has a music or art club to which you could offer your time. You don't need to think about what to say, especially if you're asking in response to 'voluntary help wanted' signs.

'Hi, I just wanted to ask you about the help you need.'

This is all it takes for them to smile, chat with you, and possibly take you up on your offer.

- **Be a good listener**

When you chat with a potential friend, use what you've learned so far to ask questions about them and listen to their answers. Look for things you have in common as they speak, and allow friendships to grow.

When you do hear something you have in common, a simple, 'Hey, I love those too!' will be all you need to make those little connections.

- **Show you're open with your body language**

How you come across physically to other people will determine whether or not you make as many friends as you'd like. So, if you are hunched over or avoiding eye contact with everyone, you won't seem like a warm person to approach.

Start with a smile, sit up a little taller, and look confident, even if it takes some time to *feel* it.

- **Make an effort**

Don't wait around for other people to invite you places or ask you questions. If you have made a friend and want to spend time together, see if they want to hang out!

A simple text can cover you for this initially, or if you pass them, you can act casually, like, 'Hey! You want to hang out on Saturday?'

It doesn't have to be a big thing; the more you ask, the easier it becomes.

- **Play a sport**

You don't have to be Serena Williams to get involved in sports. So many high school clubs are more about having fun, being active, and socializing, which is just what you're looking for! Don't be embarrassed!

You can look up different sports on YouTube and learn the rules before you get started if it makes you feel better. The good thing about playing sports is you have something to do physically to take the heat off pure conversation.

- **Learn to ask questions**

An excellent way to get people talking about themselves is by learning to ask questions.

Don't overanalyze this part; remember, it isn't an interview! Just everyday things, like, 'Did you understand this morning's assignment? I didn't really get the last part' might be good because you can either agree that you both didn't understand it and find common ground, or they can help you with what you want to know.

- **Be patient**

Friendships don't happen overnight, so don't beat yourself up if it takes weeks, or even months, to get to know someone well and feel comfortable with each other. Trust is a big idea to build, and it takes seconds to break, so that is something to bear in mind.

Use this time to reflect on how much you are growing as a person rather than thinking of it as a sprint.

- **Be a good friend to others**

Those qualities you are seeking in others? Be those qualities! There are people just like you, probably looking at you as a potential friend and wondering how to get to talk with you and build that friendship.

If you are that good friend, you'll see it returned to you. Listen well, smile, be kind, spend time together, and avoid being judgemental. People will see you as a great person, leading to real connections.

- **Make time for each other**

Good friendships are built on time and trust. If you want someone to feel loved or cared for, making time to see them is so crucial. Hang out after school, do your homework, or go on walks when the seasons change, make cookies, learn a dance, browse your social apps, and even create your own page!

7 ways to make friends quickly in school:

Making friends can be fast. Your connections with other people your age will come thick and fast, along with the opportunities to befriend them.

1. Remember to smile

As stated before, smiling is fantastic. It's instant, free, and contagious! Smiles start a lot of new friendships, and I know it can be hard to do when you feel as though you don't have any, but take a chance.

2. Names matter

There are so many ways to address people nowadays, but our names are part of us, and they matter. Calling or addressing someone by their name is an excellent way to let them know you are talking to them personally.

3. Listen to others

Everyone wants to be heard, and we all have a story. Learning to listen is key to partaking in a conversation with one or more potential friends. Know when to listen and wait for those cues to step in with something to say. Ask mostly, as we talked about before.

4. Learn the art of good convo

Know that when you do talk, it's your opportunity to be heard. You can put across your interests or thoughts, just like everybody else, and as a result, they will get to know how simply awesome you truly are.

5. Make others feel important

Is there a quality you like in another that you've picked up on? Maybe their sense of humor or the music they like. You might have seen them on social media and are a fan of their content. Let them know! It makes people feel valued when we pause and pay attention in this sometimes-crazy world.

6. Quality over quantity

Being popular and having friends doesn't mean you need to have a phone full of names and numbers. Far from it, when you find your quality of school life is way better with a few friends rather than many. Your friends reflect what you are interested in and what you value in life, so find those special few and form a team.

7. BE YOURSELF!

There is nothing worse than getting out there and pretending to be someone you aren't just because you want to fit in. What are you telling other people?

You're telling them you will be whoever they want you to be, which will erase your identity completely in the long term.

Be YOU, you can find friends who love and support that.

Nurturing connections:

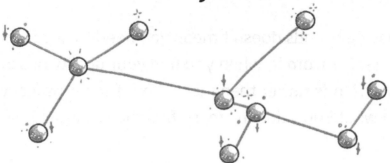

- **Support each other** – If your friend feels sad or down, you can help make them feel better by being there and listening. Ice cream always helps too!

- **Be trustworthy** – If a friend tells you a secret, maintain that confidence by keeping it to yourself.

- **Maintain respect and respectful boundaries**
  Eventually, friends argue – it's nature. It's important to respect each other and talk through any arguments you have so that you can get back on track.

- **Be polite and positive** – People generally love manners and positivity. It helps to be around those with a 'can do' attitude to life, as it can inspire others. You can be that person by tackling projects head-first and seeing the good in things, *even when your friends don't.*

- **Be honest and sincere** – Being honest doesn't mean being hurtful! But if you love something, let your friends know, and if you aren't keen on something, say, a movie, or food, it's alright to voice that.

- **Open up and be vulnerable** – People want to know you: both the good and the bad. Don't present yourself as perfect; instead, try sharing things that you find challenging. You're human!

- **Show interest in others** – Keep track of what is going on in your friends' lives and remember to ask how they're doing.

- **Keep an open mind** – Listen out for the opinions and views of your friends and look for opportunities to learn and find different perspectives within your circle.

- **Seek common ground** – Common interests are the foundation of any friendship, and there will be more over time as you get to know each other. Initially, though, seek that common ground.

- **Repair minor issues** – Fix issues when they arise rather than waiting for them to worsen! Which might mean apologizing or listening to their thoughts.

The do's and don'ts of giving advice in a friendship:

The do's :

- **Listen properly** – be the reliable ear all friends need from time to time.

- **Be encouraging** – Let your friends know they can do anything they set their minds to.

- **Involve them in your advice** – Let them see themselves in your advice so they can picture their problem being fixed.

- **Don't generalize** – Don't assume one size fits all; we are all different, and so are our opinions.

- **Question their assumptions (nicely)** – Not in a mean way, but a good friendship aims to learn from each other.

- **Look for fun new ideas** – Sometimes things don't work out, and that's alright. Always have fun and new ideas to revert to.

- **Focus on the good** – Nobody likes a Negative Nancy! Remain as upbeat as possible, although it's alright to have a bad day.

The don'ts:

- **Don't talk 'at' them** – Friends hate to be barked at, and you're not a dog. More 'with' and less 'at.'

- **Don't jump to conclusions** – Assumption is a natural killer. Keep to the facts. Surely you've heard your parents say, "to assume makes an ass out of 'u' and 'me' (eye roll); I know, but it is so true.

- **Keep the gossip to yourself** – Don't spread what you hear, especially if it's likely not true. People will begin not to trust you.

- **Don't assume you will fix things** – Some things you can't fix, but you can try to be there for the pain and sadness your friends might experience.

- **Don't judge them** – Nobody likes to be judged, especially friends.

Meet Kate, 18

Inspired by the following quote:

> *'No matter how tired I am, I get dinner at least once a
> week with my girlfriends or have a sleepover. Otherwise,
> my life is just all work.'*
>
> *– Jennifer Lawrence*

*'Every night when I go to bed, I think about what I did that day, who I saw,
and who I wish I saw but never got the time.*

*Usually, I like to keep in touch with my friends, but we are all off to college
soon, and I know we will be in different states, which will be so hard.*

*We have created a weekly Zoom meeting every Sunday afternoon, so we can
catch up, drink coffee, and be totally chill together.*

*Remembering to check in with the people in your life is so important, and I
know my friends all think the same. We don't want to lose that just because
of distance.'*

Time to reflect:

How have you been a good friend lately?

Take some time to reflect on that question and what it means to you. How have you incorporated what you've learned so far into real life, and what qualities have you offered a potential or already established friend?

You may have been a good listener or practiced the art of conversation.

_____

_____

_____

_____

_____

_____

_____

_____

Action step: Join a club or extracurricular activity

If it sounds daunting, it's because anything that encourages you out of your comfort zone should be!

Time to look at what is around your town or city and see if you can participate in something meaningful for you. That may be whatever you wish, but the outcome must be the same, get talking and see where the conversation takes you.

Action step: Create a friendship map to keep track of when you last talked with your friends and stay connected with them

Here are some great ways to set up a friendship map:

• Write the date you last talked, so you know when it's time to speak again.

• Put a number next to your friends' names, depending on your friendship level.

1. Level one can be acquaintances and people you know on a surface level.
2. Level two friends are good friends or those you keep in touch with regularly.
3. Level three friends are close friends with whom you'd be able to talk about deep, personal things.

 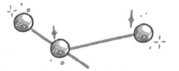

Friendship maps are an excellent reminder to stay connected!

Action step: This week, hang out with one friend or acquaintance outside of school.

A big one, perhaps! But totally feasible. You can do it, and you know you can. I bet someone wants to hang out with you equally as badly as you want to ask them – so go for it!

You may want to hang out at the park or go to the movies and have some ice cream so you can talk about the movie you saw. It may be as simple as an after-school walk home. Either way, do what works for you!

How do you feel?

You deserve to be selective with your friendships, and just because you may not have many, it doesn't mean you have to pick the first person you see.

Not all friendships are healthy or give us the things that we *need*, like the feeling of trust and appreciation.

In making real friends, you don't need to hold onto every connection you make with just anybody.

That being said, it is time to dive into toxic friendships and what they look like (I am sure you have had or have seen a few!)

Chapter 6

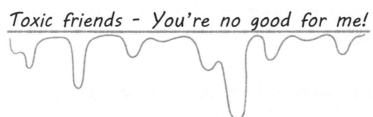

Toxic friends - You're no good for me!

Not all friendships are equal. Sometimes you can be on the receiving end of some really toxic behavior from those who claim to be your friend.

It can be challenging to tell when you're in a one-sided or toxic friendship, but as you start to see your worth, you might notice your existing relationships aren't as healthy as you thought.

So, what can you do about it?

What are toxic, one-sided, and co-dependent friendships?

Toxic friendships

Toxic friendships tend to produce feelings of anxiety, stress, and sadness. Instead of feeling happy, they can make you feel drained or even, in some cases, unsafe.

Your friend might belittle you often or criticize you and make you feel stupid. These friendships can make you feel alone and bring you down, and you'll likely be the one left blaming yourself for their behavior as your self-confidence and self-esteem dwindles.

One-sided friendships

If one person puts way more work into the friendship than the other to uphold it, you're looking at a one-sided friendship.

How do you know if you're in a one-sided friendship?

- You always have to initiate doing things, or you'll never see them.
- You always have to go to their place; they won't come to you.
- You support them but don't see it returned when you need them.
- You help them but get nothing back.
- They only talk about themselves and never ask about you.

Sometimes people are genuinely busy, but you need to trust your instincts and learn whether or not they are just making excuses.

Everyone has homework, but are they always 'doing homework?' If so, it may be a sign that they're just not putting in the effort, especially if they make time for other friends.

Co-dependent friendships

Co-dependent friendships lack boundaries. What happens is that you and your friend become so dependent on each other that you lose complete touch with your own needs and feelings.

You lose your identity, eventually leading to problems within the friendship. You might rely on one friend for all your needs, which is a huge responsibility for them, or vice versa.

You could also give up other friendships, hobbies, or interests for this one friendship or be jealous if one or the other spends time with another friend. The worst part can be when you feel anxious or stressed if you don't see or talk to your friend for a while.

How to identify them

So, what can you look out for on your journey toward making friends?

What does an unhealthy friendship look like?

Unhealthy friends tend to come to you when they want something, good or bad.

You might feel your boundaries aren't respected, and potentially your time and feelings too. That could involve bullying, teasing, or putting you down in front of others to make themselves look better.

Unhealthy friendships leave the other person drained, and the friendship, in general, will likely be one-sided as you're there for them but not the other way around – and that can suck!

You might notice their apologies seem _insincere_ and almost _sarcastic_, and their regular habit of making you feel nervous or unsettled will likely start getting to you big time. They will unapologetically gossip about anyone they can to make their lives more interesting. Remember – they want to be liked.

If you feel as though you're changing, it could be that they are the ones pulling those strings. Over time, they want to mold you to their liking so that you become totally reliant on them. That may mean they compare you to others, designed to make you feel horrible about yourself, usually to get you to do what they want.

They think they and their needs come first, and you will either have to like it or dump it.

Signs of a toxic friend:

- **They're always 'one-up' on you** – Whatever they do always has to be BIGGER, **better**, and more *expensive*!
- **They're a terrible influence** – Perhaps they try to entice you over to their dark side, as they see you keen to please and encourage you to do things that aren't like you.
- **They bully and belittle you** – To assert control and let you know that they're the *leaders* of the friendship, they will do what it takes to put you in your place and make you look small or irrelevant.
- **You lose your self-esteem** – Your wonderful character will erode, and you'll wonder what happened to the girl you used to know. It's like giving up your energy supply to someone else and being left with nothing.

Signs of a co-dependent friend:

- **One person always needs rescuing** – There is always one person in the friendship who is more reliant on the other. There is another word for it – needy.
- **One person spends a lot of time trying to fix the other's problems** – This unbalances the friendship scales, and one person gets more care, attention, and advice than the other.
- **One person always feels exhausted after hanging out** – Yep – and usually, the one who has had to listen to all of the other's problems and stressors. But the problem is, they are reliant on you to listen, and you are attached to the idea of being wanted and needed. It's totally unhealthy.
- **You mirror feelings** – Rather than be your own keeper of your thoughts and emotions or go against each other sometimes, as all humans do, you pair up all the time. Happy/happy, sad/sad, excited/excited. Who are you underneath it all?

Red flags in relationships (both romantic and platonic)

What things can you look out for when it comes to making friends?

- **Overly controlling behavior** – Do they have the last word or tell you what to wear, what to do or not to do? These are just some examples of overly controlling behavior.

- **Feeling low** – People in your friendship circle should be building you up, not knocking you down.

- **Physical or mental abuse** – These are undeniable red flags for any kind of 'ship.' Physical abuse is very straightforward and obvious, but it's harder to spot the signs of emotional abuse when it can happen for weeks, months, or even years. None of it, I repeat none, is right.

- **Substance abuse** – This shows your friend struggles with impulse control and self-destructive habits. Quickly leading to addiction in many cases; you should reach out for help if you spot this in a friend. A teacher or parent would be a good place to start.

- **Narcissism** – Narcissists believe the world revolves around them and is a serious mental condition that cannot be diagnosed often due to the person in question being in total denial. Once you spot one, you can know what to look out for – and avoid!

- **Anger management issues** – This type of person can make you feel unsafe and is straight-up toxic behavior.

- **Inability to resolve conflict** – People need to take responsibility, and if they choose to walk away, it's a sign they don't want the conflict in their lives. This is not healthy.

- **Constant jealousy** – If a friend is constantly jealous of you, it shows they care more about what they want than your happiness.

- **Gaslighting** - it's a really mean way to manipulate someone, and it can drive people insane! If a friend is like, 'No, that didn't happen,' and you remember that it did, their argument can make you question your memory and doubt yourself. Huge red flag!

- **Pulling you away from family and other friends** – Those who isolate you do not have your best interests at heart. You cannot and should not rely on one person's friendship alone, and they shouldn't expect that of you either.

Toxic traits – what to spot

Toxic friends create negative vibes. They use their voice to be judgemental or just plain rude. It isn't like they don't mean to; they get a kick out of seeing people respond to them like they enjoy any attention, even if it's negative attention.

When you think you're having a good day, toxic friends can see the boredom in the peace and rile up their so-called friends by picking arguments, blowing hot and cold, or asserting their bossiness into the moment.

People with toxic traits tend to go for the kinder, more empathic friend because they can easily manipulate them and know they will always be forgiven for their behavior. It doesn't make you weak; it makes them sneaky and dishonest.

They aren't <u>thoughtful; they are pretty darn greedy and self-centered</u>. They have zero self-awareness, don't see fault in themselves, and are critical and thoughtless.

Of course, they can be nice when they want to be, which draws people back to them. Put plainly, toxic friends suck the life out of you, and they use that life to fuel their own needs.

What to do about them

You have control, whether you believe it or not! You can decide who _you_ want in your life without feeling guilty about your choices.

Before it gets to the point of no return, you can think about ways to approach their behavior.

What to do about toxic friendships:

1. **Confront them** – Your friend may not even realize they're being toxic. If you think that's the case, talk to them and tell them how you feel. Their response will be what you need to look out for because if they throw it back at you, they aren't taking responsibility for how they've made you feel.

2. **Stay away** – With a bit of space, you can see how your life changes. Is it for the better?

3. **Accept how you feel** – Avoiding someone you once cared for is difficult. You'll likely feel guilty. Just accept how you feel and let whatever emotions come and go so you can move on.

4. **Take your time** – You might feel a little lonely if you cut the friendship, but you will return to your usual self. Don't be forced back to the situation you walked away from, though – keep it in the past!

What to do about one-sided friendships:

1. **Talk to them** – As much as it is a good idea to speak to them, it's usually ineffective because they will be used to having things their way.

2. **Cut the tie** – This is quite hard to do if you value the friendship. It shows you have a kind heart, so try to be consistent with this and keep to your choice.

3. **Grow your social circle** – This is a great long-term solution because you will grow your friend circle and do a lot of growing and learning along the way. It's a tremendous problem-solving skill as well!

What to do about co-dependent friendships:

1. **Recognize the issue** – What is lacking in your life that you rely on your friend so much? Did something happen to make you feel you have nobody else?

2. **Learn how to take care of yourself** – Remember that you matter and take the time to learn ways to feel good and practice some self-care rituals.

3. **Give more, take less** – Being the one who takes all the time can leave the other feeling exhausted. Try to remember to be the one to offer yourself sometimes.

What if someone is co-dependent on you?

Firstly, you need to figure out how you got to this place. What attracted you to the friendship, and is deeper work at play here? Is this a regular thing for you?

Practicing putting yourself first is a great way to apply boundaries which can be challenging initially. Although it seems scary, it will teach you a lot about yourself and your friend if they respond poorly to you saying no occasionally.

You'd better be prepared for a major shift/change, though! You may not make people happy as you become more assertive, but those who love you and honestly want your friendship will totally understand.

How to end a friendship

This can be tricky, but if you really need to end a toxic friendship, there are signs to look out for and ways to do it.

Is it time to end a friendship?

Step 1: Determine how you feel and what you want

Will your friend change if you tell them how you're feeling? Your friend might be busy at the moment and completely unaware they are hurting you. Would they be apologetic if you spoke to them?

- What **can** you control?

You can control how you respond to their toxic behavior. That's when those boundaries come in handy!

- What **can't** you control?

You can't control what they do or say. Sadly, they will act how they want to, including being hurtful to the point where you question the friendship.

Step 2: Have a conversation

This doesn't have to be a huge thing! Confrontation sucks, so it's good to go in gently but ensure you get your feelings across.

If it helps – write it down. You can think carefully about what you want to say, and they can read it in their own time and space. You can even say that you're a little nervous about talking and that you'd appreciate it if they were patient with you.

Step 3: Set new boundaries

Reduce contact or take a break – This is self-explanatory; give yourself some space to think and breathe. You can reassess appropriately with a clear mind.

Step 4: If the previous steps don't work, end the friendship

- Fade them out – Begin to start doing things on your own or with other people. This should be gradual so that it seems as though nature is taking its course.

- Officially end the friendship - It's a bold step, but you can be honest and say you don't feel things are working out in your friendship but wish them well.

- Completely drop them – If you are at the point where you have begun to see your worth for the weight in gold it is, ditch them and save your sanity.

Step 5: Get support from your other friends and loved ones, and practice self-care

This is a healing part of any friendship recovery because it involves prioritizing yourself. Look for support from friends and family, but avoid gossiping or bad-mouthing the person too much. You want a clean slate and not to get bogged down by further negativity.

Meet Hilary, 22

Inspired by the following quote:

> *'It's not healthy to stay with people that*
> *don't even bother to ask how you are.'*
> *- Unknown*

'I had a friend at school who was so awesome at first. She made me feel really good about myself, to the point where all I wanted to do was hang out with her. A few girls warned me about her, saying she talked about me behind my back, but I stupidly stood up for my friend.

It got to the point where I was beginning to not feel like myself anymore, and as my confidence began to disappear, she would tease me or laugh at my hairstyle, what clothes I wore, or the music I liked. It was always about her and her needs, and anything that went wrong was immediately my fault.

My parents noticed the change and asked me what was going on, and as I explained, it was clear that I had a toxic friendship. I felt totally lost and so unhappy and insecure. Meanwhile, she was never better.

My advice to anyone experiencing the same would be to talk to someone you trust outside of school to help you get a clear picture of what's happening.'

Meet Ashley, 21

Inspired by the following quote:

> 'Beauty begins the moment you decide to be yourself'
> – Coco Chanel

'I found it hard to admit that my friend was pretty toxic. I saw this person who had been in my life for so long that I was kind of in denial that she would hurt me.

The day came when another friend stopped talking to me for no reason, and when I dug a little deeper, I found out it was because she was told I said some really horrible things about her when actually it was my toxic friend.

At that point, I'd had enough. I spoke to this person, who naturally denied everything, but I could tell by her body language that she was lying, so I phased her out and regained some of the old friends I had lost before this event.

I would advise anyone going through something similar to just walk away. Toxic friends aren't worth the hassle in the long run, but you can only appreciate the freedom if you have experienced the toxicity!'

Is it time to ditch?

This toxic friendship quiz will help you assess your relationships and decide whether they are toxic or not.

10 questions – the more 'yes' answers you get – the more toxic the friendship is!

1   They like drama
    yes or **no**

2   Arguing with them is a nightmare
    yes or **no**

3   You feel insecure around them
    yes or **no**

4   You often think life would be better without them in it
    yes or **no**

5   They tell you they're like family to you, and family comes first
    yes or **no**

6   It's never their fault
    yes or **no**

7   It's hard for them to be happy for you
    yes or **no**

8   They embarrass you
    yes or **no**

9   You never feel heard around them
    yes or **no**

10 They totally flip for no reason
    yes or **no**

How do you feel?

Toxicity is everywhere, but this chapter should have made you realize that you can spot those traits and do something about them before you get caught up in friendships that aren't healthy.

Hopefully, you don't realize that you may also be carrying some toxic traits. There are *so* many opportunities in this book for self-reflection that will help you address any negative habits you may be holding on to so you can keep your slate clean moving forward.

With those negative habits affecting the people around us, it's time to learn that there is so much you can do to erase those too!

Chapter 7

I got this! Changing negative habits.

Well, here we are, on the final stretch of your journey of learning about friendships. How has it been for you, and what resonates with you the most?

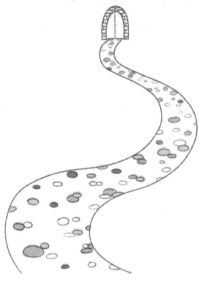

The concept of making friends is supported by having great social habits, but sometimes these take time to recognize. This might be due to having more negative social patterns that prevent us from being the best version of ourselves.

Let's run through these and find ways to start working on changing them today.

How to change your life

Nothing this big is easy or quick. Wanting something overnight and being frustrated that you aren't winning is so common, but makeovers are way more than just styling your hair differently and getting new clothes.

It involves doing something we all hate to do when we feel low – taking a good look at ourselves!

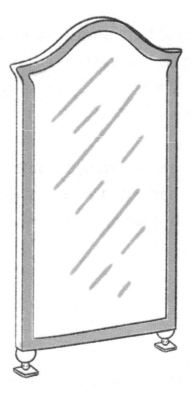

Changing your thoughts

Before any emotion you feel or action you take, comes a thought. If we had different thoughts, we would see those emotions and actions change.

Say I want to start making friends. Before I start, I have to have the thought that I want to. Emotions come after that thought, but that thought has to be positive for the emotion to be! Shifting your thoughts will help this process.

Change how you think – don't downplay your abilities

An excellent way to think about starting to change your mindset is by remembering you can do it. Your current habits do not define you, nor are you trapped by them!

It would be best if you believed that you can change – that is the key. If you don't, then you won't even bother trying.

What is a growth mindset?

The growth mindset is a total buzz phrase that everyone is starting to use. It means to feel the fear but do it anyway because it's the only way we grow. If we stay in our comfort zones, we aren't learning anything new or trying new ways to deal with issues we have.

It's about knowing things can go wrong but not letting those things stop us from trying. Sometimes we feel bad when we make mistakes or when something doesn't work in our favor, but we figure out what makes us feel inadequate and work to improve it for next time.

Change your expectations

If you can start seeing positive change in your mind and preparing yourself for it, rather than the usual image of failure or doubt, you will be far more likely to get what you want. It's like taking a good thought and planting it like a seed. It will only grow if you water it.

Changing your emotions

You know those negative emotions you feel when facing something scary or nerve-wracking; you can change them! Remember we talked about challenging negative thoughts previously? This is a great example of putting those tips to good use.

Practicing gratitude should never be underrated. Like we talked about with the journal and thinking of things you appreciate on a daily basis. Your thoughts and emotions will slowly but surely change for the better.

Find motivation to change.

It's hard to be motivated and even harder to motivate yourself, especially if you feel low or worthless.

You can start small, though! Try these few tips to get you motivated in general:

- Keep your room tidy, cleaning it regularly
- Help with the dishes after dinner
- Spend time looking after your pets, if you have any, with walking or feeding

They may seem silly, but they are an excellent catalyst for bigger things, and those bigger things will become more manageable.

Think about the following when you are trying to motivate yourself:

- Doing something without being asked
- Wanting to achieve something big or small
- Being committed to what you want
- Being resilient on those more brutal days
- The desire to try new things and keep improving

Visualize your potential future

These following words might help you visualize the future you:

1.	Adventurous	5.	Confident
2.	Ambitious	6.	Enthusiastic
3.	Capable	7.	Loyal
4.	Courageous	8.	Open

Sounds great, doesn't it? It could be *you*!

10 common negative social habits and what to do about them

1. **Seeking attention by complaining**
   Constantly talking about everything wrong in your life can be exhausting for everyone, including you. It's a poor way to keep someone's attention. Talk about what you're grateful for, not what's bothering you.

2. **Focusing on what you want to say next instead of listening**
   You can blow a conversation by thinking about what you want to say next instead of just staying in the moment and actually listening to what someone is saying. Practice active listening, and you'll improve so much.

3. **Multi-tasking while you talk to someone**
   It just makes you look plain rude and not interested if you aren't giving someone your full attention by looking at your phone or the TV.

4. **Not paying attention to the people you care about**
   People who know you well can tell if your heart isn't in the conversation. They want you to be sincere, so give them your love by listening intently.

5. **Fishing for compliments**
   This is super unflattering and kind of annoying when people pick up on people who always look for compliments.
   Know your worth and stop relying on other people for constant validation.

6. **Undermining compliments with self-deprecating comments**
   If someone says something nice to you, it's OK to say thank you! You don't have to bring your ego to the party, nor do you have to bat it away; smile, say thanks, and move on.

7. **Cutting people off mid-sentence**
   Don't command attention by making everything about you. Value their thoughts and words.

   Sometimes you may need to cut people off, such as in an emergency, but your job is to be aware of when it is appropriate.

8. **Being unsupportive**
   Letting people know you care is a beautiful thing. Express it often! Approach every conversation with empathy and compassion for the other person.

9. **Trying to please everyone**
   Stay sane by being yourself and not what everyone wants you to be. You cannot please everyone. You are not a jar of Nutella. Practice prioritizing your own needs.

10. **Looking like you don't want to be there**
    Body language is a visual book everyone can read. Give off good vibes, and you'll attract good attention.

    Chapter 4 can be revisited for body language tips.

Meet Kory, 19

Inspired by the following quote:

"The greatest discovery of all time is that a person can change his future by merely changing his attitude"

- Oprah Winfrey

'I was so shy in high school. Nothing would get me talking to people because I was petrified of making or even maintaining a conversation with anyone. I made any excuse to play on my phone.

I used to scroll social media, look on Twitter, or even check the weather in different parts of the world to avoid talking to people!

It got so bad I started doing it at home and around my family, and they got pretty annoyed with me, thinking I didn't care or didn't want to be around them.

It wasn't the case, but I didn't see how my phone habit kinda took over everything.

It was my safety net, though.

I started to be on it less around my family at first, which gave me the confidence to start chatting more and more. Eventually, I used it to make conversation, like, 'hey, check out this tweet,' to the person next to me in class. It became a segue for conversation, and I didn't need to do that at all after a while.'

Meet Bella, 22

Inspired by the following quote:

'Be a good person in real life, not on social media'
- Unknown

'I used to be so insecure, like majorly not good enough. However, school was the worst because you're there with like a thousand other kids who all seem better than you at everything.

I used to hate conversations with people because I would finish sentences for people or cut them off mid-way. They'd be telling a cool story, and I'd guess what they would say and get it in before they had a chance. Looking back, I think I did it to try and fit in. To prove that I was on their wavelength or something. I wanted to be liked, but one day a girl on my volleyball team told me I always cut her off, and I was so embarrassed.

I always remembered that I could just shut down and not have any friends, or I could do something about it, so I tried to be aware when anyone else spoke to me and waited until they finished before I said what I wanted to say.

It was hard; I mean, it was a habit I built but ended up hating, but I did change, and I was so much better after, knowing I was being annoying.

Habits are super easy to start and so hard to break, but I did it because my choices were sink or swim!'

Time to reflect!

This final assessment allows you to see if you have a growth or fixed mindset.

If your score does not leave you feeling confident about the health of your mindset, it will at least be able to show you areas in which you can work toward a growth mindset.

There are 15 questions, each scoring similarly to assessments from previous chapters, from 0 through 5. (0 being not at all, 5 being definitely).

1. No matter how much you know something, there is always more room to learn about it

    0   1   2   3   4   5

2. I like my schoolwork the best when it makes me think hard

    0   1   2   3   4   5

3. I like to be challenged at school and find hard work quite fun

    0   1   2   3   4   5

4. I love making mistakes because I learn from them and improve

    0   1   2   3   4   5

5. Intelligence is earned, and if I want to learn something, I will

    0   1   2   3   4   5

6. I like receiving feedback because it tells me where I need to make improvements so I can perform better

    0   1   2   3   4   5

7. I'm happy to try new things because it always results in meeting new people

    0   1   2   3   4   5

8. I think it's possible we can be whoever we want to be

    0   1   2   3   4   5

9. If I sniff out any bad habits in myself, I find it easy to fix them

    0   1   2   3   4   5

10. I get scared sometimes, but I never let it stop me from doing what I love

    0   1   2   3   4   5

11. If my parents ask me to help around the house, I am happy to do so

    0   1   2   3   4   5

12. The more I speak to people, the easier it becomes

    0   1   2   3   4   5

13. I see fear as a process that I have the tools to work through

    0   1   2   3   4   5

14. I love meeting new people

    0   1   2   3   4   5

15. If I have a terrible day, I am very resilient and know that tomorrow will be better

    0   1   2   3   4   5

0-12 - Strong fixed mindset

13-28 - Fixed with some growth ideas

29-45 - Growth with some fixed ideas

46-75 - Stronger growth mindset (the higher the score, the stronger the growth mindset).

How did you feel answering those questions? Sometimes, everything we're going through seems quite manageable until we see it in black and white.

_____

_____

_____

_____

_____

When faced with what we don't like (your answers may have raised some negative concerns), Instead of using it as your 'rock bottom,' treat it as the foundation from which your confidence can grow and your habits can, and will, change.

How do you feel?

Trying to improve yourself is a constant process. As you grow, you'll want to try new ways to improve, which can get pretty tiring sometimes. It's so worth it though!

Your life will be richer and *so* much more fulfilling, and so will your friendships if you learn to take the time to dig out those old habits and replace them with shiny new ones.

Being aware of them is the critical first step!

In all the ways you think you're not good enough or cannot do many things, you did something fantastic in reading this book.

Each chapter in this book has been like a stepping stone toward a better, more confident life for yourself. One that involves making and keeping the right friends and having the ideas and encouragement to do so.

It's cool to get to the end and feel like you've done something for yourself, right?

You've gone from learning what anxiety is in the beginning, to thinking about changing how you approach opportunities that will benefit you and everything in between.

What was your favorite chapter, and why?

Was there a particular interactive element that made you go, 'ohhh! I get it now!'?

This book is like a journey, and as you've gone along, you've learned how to deal, or not deal, with certain aspects of making friends. Not only that, but you've also learned who the heck to stay away from and why.

The tools you now have are significantly more than you did when you first started reading, and they will help you move forward in all kinds of social situations.

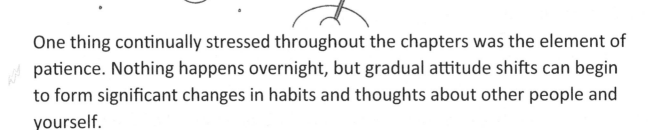

One thing continually stressed throughout the chapters was the element of patience. Nothing happens overnight, but gradual attitude shifts can begin to form significant changes in habits and thoughts about other people and yourself.

With each chapter came action steps and moments to reflect. Hearing from real-life young women who have been through the exact thing you're going through should help you see that there is an end to feeling the way you do and that managing anxiety, learning to control your emotions, and building self-esteem will help you form friendships that will last a lifetime.

The final story I wanted to share with you is the best one yet. This young lady came to me personally when she heard I was writing this book because she knew it resonated with her and her high school memories. Her name is Natalie, and she has this final message to share with you:

Meet Natalie, 23

'My father is in the military, and we changed schools a lot as kids. I was the oldest of 3 siblings, so it was up to me to lead the way, which was really intimidating and made me feel super anxious.

We ended up at a school in Oklahoma, and I did what I usually do; go there knowing it won't last long before we moved again. The knowledge of continuously moving soon became my safety net, so I never bothered making real friends until we landed here. My father told us this was where I would be until I graduated, which was two more years.

Naturally, I freaked out because it meant I had to stay long enough to get to know people, which was something I had never done.

I developed terrible anxiety and was self-conscious. I knew nobody, but I knew I couldn't carry on that way.
Eventually, a teacher noticed I could draw well and suggested I help out with the drama club, designing the props.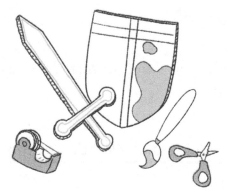
I said yes because it was something I could happily do alone, but another girl my age, Tiffany, was doing the same as me.

We spent a lot of time together, and it took us so long to chat as we were both shy.

Eventually, we did, and we became inseparable. We also ended up attending the same art college where we majored together and started our own illustration company.

Looking back, I was petrified. I had to stick around and be vulnerable, but I did it, and I came out with a friend for life.

My advice is just to be yourself. Making friends doesn't have to be a terrible thing. Don't go out looking for ten friends; start small and look for quality.

You can do it!'

Like Natalie says, making friends doesn't have to feel like pulling teeth! You can learn to shut the nagging voice inside your head up with the practical strategies in this book and create genuine, uplifting friendships.

In the end, if you loved this book and want to share it with others, it would be fantastic if you left an honest review. Your review would mean the word is spreading, and we can help other girls who have felt just like you together! Let's encourage those who need this book to pick up a copy and start making real friendships today.

You never know – eventually, you might write your story in someone's book someday!

Take care and good luck. You got this!

A SHORT NOTE FROM TRUE TEENZ

We hope you truly enjoyed this workbook!

True Teenz is dedicated to helping and educating teens to better their life, communication, social, and relationship skills.

We would love to hear your honest thoughts on the book. If you could take just 60 seconds to write a short review on Amazon, it would be greatly appreciated. Scan the QR code below to leave a review.

If you would like to share a success story, we would love to hear it! Please send an email to hello@trueteenz.com.

TRUE TEENZ
PUBLISHING

REFERENCES

7 Active Listening Techniques to Practice in Your Daily Conversations. (2022, September 15). Verywell Mind. Retrieved October 14, 2022, from https://www.verywellmind.com/what-is-active-listening-3024343

Advice on Friendship: How to Give and Receive Advice. (n.d.). Retrieved October 14, 2022, from https://www.betterup.com/blog/advice-on-friendship?hs_preview=IGsVerHj-70339777188

Agarwal, A. (2021, December 5). 4 Ways To Deal With That Toxic Friend & End All Ties Without Hurting Them. www.mensxp.com. Retrieved October 14, 2022, from https://www.mensxp.com/relationships/friendship/97328-how-to-deal-with-a-toxic-friend.html

Anxiety (for Teens) - Nemours KidsHealth. (n.d.). Retrieved October 14, 2022, from https://kidshealth.org/en/teens/anxiety.html

Anxiety Canada. (2022, October 7). How to ride out intense emotions. Retrieved October 14, 2022, from https://www.anxietycanada.com/articles/riding-out-intense-emotions/

Aswell, S. (2020, August 20). I Use This 5-Minute Therapy Technique Every Day for My Anxiety. Healthline. Retrieved October 14, 2022, from https://www.healthline.com/health/mental-health/self-talk-exercises

9 BAD SOCIAL HABITS YOU SHOULD BREAK TODAY. (2016, October 11). eL CREMA. Retrieved October 14, 2022, from https://www.elcrema.com/9-bad-social-habits-you-should-break-today/

B.Sc., S. B. V. A., B.Sc., S. B. V. A., B.Sc., S. B. V. A., Morin, D. A., Morin, D. A., Morin, D. A., Morin, D. A., Morin, D. A., Morin, D. A., & Morin, D. A. (2022, August 19). How to Make Friends (Meet, Befriend, and Bond). SocialSelf. Retrieved October 14, 2022, from https://socialself.com/blog/how-to-make-new-friends/

B.Sc., S. B. V. A., Morin, D. A., Morin, D. A., B.Sc., S. B. V. A., Morin, D. A., Morin, D. A., B.Sc., S. B. V. A., Morin, D. A., Morin, D. A., B.Sc., S. B. V. A., B.Sc., S. B. V. A., Ashfield, C., & Morin, D. A. (2022, March 22). How to have a conversation without asking too many questions. SocialSelf. Retrieved October 14, 2022, from https://socialself.com/blog/make-conversation/

B.Sc., S. B. V. A., Morin, D. A., Morin, D. A., Morin, D. A., B.Sc., S. B. V. A., B.Sc., S. B. V. A., B.Sc., S. B. V. A., B.Sc., S. B. V. A., B.Sc., S. B. V. A., B.Sc., S. B. V. A., Morin, D. A., B.Sc., S. B. V. A., B.Sc., S. B. V. A., B.Sc., S. B. V. A., B.Sc., S. B. V. A., B.Sc., S. B. V. A., Morin, D. A., & Haworth, A. (2022, March 1). 222 Questions to Get to Know Someone (Casual to Personal). SocialSelf. Retrieved October 14, 2022, from https://socialself.com/blog/questions-to-get-to-know-someone/

Belmont, M. J. S. (2017, July 25). CBT Technique: Using the Triple Column Technique to Change Your Thoughts To Change Your Life! Psych Central. Retrieved October 14, 2022, from https://psychcentral.com/pro/psychoeducation/2017/07/cbt-technique-using-the-triple-column-technique-to-change-your-thoughts-to-change-your-life

Bennett, T., Bennett, T., Bennett, T., Centore, A., PhD, Bennett, T., Bennett, T., Negroni, J., Bambini, M., Bennett, T., Centore, A., PhD, Bennett, T., & Crosby, J. (2022, August 18). How to deal with toxic friends. Thriveworks. Retrieved October 14, 2022, from https://thriveworks.com/blog/how-to-deal-with-toxic-friends/

Bertone, H. C. J. (2019, October 2). Which Type of Meditation Is Right for Me? Healthline. Retrieved October 14, 2022, from https://www.healthline.com/health/mental-health/types-of-meditation

Bezzy Depression. (n.d.). Retrieved October 14, 2022, from https://www.bezzydepression.com/discover/dep-self-care/health-mood-journal-101-how-to-get-started-on-controlling-your-emotions?-

Body Language: Beyond Words – How to Read Unspoken Signals. (n.d.). Mind Tools. Retrieved October 14, 2022, from https://www.mindtools.com/pages/article/Body_Language.htm

Can Self-Compassion Make You Happier? (2020, December 28). Verywell Mind. Retrieved October 14, 2022, from https://www.verywellmind.com/can-self-compassion-make-you-happier-4159536

Casabianca, S. S. (2021, July 29). 9 Tips to Change Negative Thinking. Psych Central. Retrieved October 14, 2022, from https://psychcentral.com/lib/fixing-cognitive-distortions

Casabianca, S. S. (2022, January 11). 15 Cognitive Distortions To Blame for Negative Thinking. Psych Central. Retrieved October 14, 2022, from https://psychcentral.com/lib/cognitive-distortions-negative-thinking

Chen, J. P. (2020, September 20). Mindfulness of Emotions -- The Manhattan Center for CBT. Manhattan Center for Cognitive Behavioral Therapy. Retrieved October 14, 2022, from https://www.manhattancbt.com/archives/489/mindfulness-of-emotions/

Chill Out: How to Use Progressive Muscle Relaxation to Quell Anxiety. (2020, August 3). Verywell Mind. Retrieved October 14, 2022, from https://www.verywellmind.com/how-do-i-practice-progressive-muscle-relaxation-3024400

Chill Out: How to Use Progressive Muscle Relaxation to Quell Anxiety. (2020b, August 3). Verywell Mind. Retrieved October 14, 2022, from https://www.verywellmind.com/how-do-i-practice-progressive-muscle-relaxation-3024400

Colorado State University Global. (2021, May 10). What is Active Listening? 4 Tips for Improving Communication Skills. Retrieved October 14, 2022, from https://csuglobal.edu/blog/what-active-listening-4-tips-improving-communication-skills

3 Coping Strategies That Actually Make Social Anxiety Worse. (2020, May 28). Verywell Mind. Retrieved October 14, 2022, from https://www.verywellmind.com/what-are-avoidance-behaviors-3024312

Could Anxiety Actually Have an Upside in Your Life? (2020, November 21). Verywell Mind. Retrieved October 14, 2022, from https://www.verywellmind.com/the-purpose-of-anxiety-2797497

Cronkleton, E. (2019, April 9). 10 Breathing Techniques for Stress Relief and More. Healthline. Retrieved October 14, 2022, from https://www.healthline.com/health/breathing-exercise

editor. (2020, July 2). Importance Of Social Media Etiquette For Teens. Lagosmums. Retrieved October 14, 2022, from https://lagosmums.com/importance-of-social-media-etiquette-for-teens/

Edwards, V. van. (2022, July 12). 10 Action Steps to Become a Good Friend. Science of People. Retrieved October 14, 2022, from https://www.scienceofpeople.com/good-friend/

Edwards, V. van. (2022a, May 24). Want to Change Your Life? Use These 13 Science-Backed Tips. Science of People. Retrieved October 14, 2022, from https://www.scienceofpeople.com/how-to-change/

Effective Communication. (n.d.). HelpGuide.org. Retrieved October 14, 2022, from https://www.helpguide.org/articles/relationships-communication/effective-communication.htm

Eizenberg, I. (2019, August 13). Test Yourself: Are You in a Toxic Friendship? Playbuzz. Retrieved October 14, 2022, from https://www.playbuzz.com/innaeizenberg10/test-yourself-are-you-in-a-toxic-friendship

Emotions and Types of Emotional Responses. (2022, February 25). Verywell Mind. Retrieved October 14, 2022, from https://www.verywellmind.com/what-are-emotions-2795178

Estrada, J. (2021, September 19). How To Accept Compliments & Why It's So Hard For Some. The Zoe Report. Retrieved October 14, 2022, from https://www.thezoereport.com/wellness/how-to-accept-compliments-graciously

findcourses.com. (2020, February 10). Communication Skills Assessment - Test Yourself! Retrieved October 14, 2022, from https://www.findcourses.com/prof-dev/quizzes/communication-skills-assessment-17666

Friendships: Enrich your life and improve your health. (2022, January 12). Mayo Clinic. Retrieved October 14, 2022, from https://www.mayoclinic.org/healthy-lifestyle/adult-health/in-depth/friendships/art-20044860

Geller, C. P. (2020, September 20). Why You Have Intense Emotions, and How to Cope - Manhattan CBT. Manhattan Center for Cognitive Behavioral Therapy. Retrieved October 14, 2022, from https://www.manhattancbt.com/archives/1991/intense-emotions/

Greene, P. (2022, May 23). 9 Critical Mindfulness Tips for Those Just Starting Out -. Manhattan Center for Cognitive Behavioral Therapy. Retrieved October 14, 2022, from https://www.manhattancbt.com/mindfulness-tips/

Griffin, T. (2020, December 6). We Need to Talk More About Codependency in Friendships. Essence. Retrieved October 14, 2022, from https://www.essence.com/lifestyle/health-wellness/we-need-to-talk-more-about-codependency-in-friendships/

Gross, E. L. (2022, May 18). 10 Signs Your Friendship Is Toxic, and How To Deal With It. Well+Good. Retrieved October 14, 2022, from https://www.wellandgood.com/signs-of-toxic-friendship/

Healthy Coping Skills for Uncomfortable Emotions. (2022, September 6). Verywell Mind. Retrieved October 14, 2022, from https://www.verywellmind.com/forty-healthy-coping-skills-4586742

Healthy Self-Esteem vs. Low Self-Esteem. (2022, July 24). Calmerry -. Retrieved October 14, 2022, from https://us.calmerry.com/blog/self-esteem/signs-of-healthy-and-low-self-esteem/

Healthy Self-Esteem vs. Low Self-Esteem. (2022b, July 24). Calmerry -. Retrieved October 14, 2022, from https://us.calmerry.com/blog/self-esteem/signs-of-healthy-and-low-self-esteem/

How Anxiety Affects Relationships. (2022, June 6). Verywell Mind. Retrieved October 14, 2022, from https://www.verywellmind.com/how-anxiety-can-cause-relationship-problems-1393090

How Good Are Your Communication Skills?: – Speaking, Listening, Writing, and Reading Effectively. (n.d.). Mind Tools. Retrieved October 14, 2022, from https://www.mindtools.com/pages/article/newCS_99.htm

How Thought Stopping Works to Banish Negative Thinking. (2021, June 25). Verywell Mind. Retrieved October 14, 2022, from https://www.verywellmind.com/what-is-thought-stopping-and-how-does-it-work-2584122

How to Be a Good Friend. (2021, August 30). WebMD. Retrieved October 14, 2022, from https://www.webmd.com/balance/features/how-be-good-friend

How to Break Up With a Toxic Friend. (2021, August 31). WebMD. Retrieved October 14, 2022, from https://www.webmd.com/balance/features/toxic-friends-less-friend-more-foe

How to Change: 6 Science-Based Tips & Strategies. (n.d.). The Berkeley Well-Being Institute. Retrieved October 14, 2022, from https://www.berkeleywellbeing.com/how-to-change.html

How To End A Conversation | www.succeedsocially.com. (n.d.). Retrieved October 14, 2022, from https://www.succeedsocially.com/endconversations

How To Make Friends at School: 7 Proven Ways. (2021, August 2). Jonny Shannon. Retrieved October 14, 2022, from https://www.jonnyshannon.com/blog/7-proven-ways-to-make-friends-quickly-in-high-school

How to Make Friends in High School | Cappex. (n.d.). Retrieved October 14, 2022, from https://www.cappex.com/articles/academics/how-to-make-friends-in-high-school

How to make new friends. (n.d.). Retrieved October 14, 2022, from https://www.kidscape.org.uk/advice/advice-for-young-people/friendships-and-frenemies/how-to-make-new-friends/

How to overcome your shyness. (n.d.). Meeting New People | ReachOut Australia. Retrieved October 14, 2022, from https://au.reachout.com/articles/how-to-overcome-your-shyness

How to Stop Negative Thoughts that Cause Anxiety | Calmerry. (2022, July 13). Calmerry -. Retrieved October 14, 2022, from https://us.calmerry.com/blog/therapy/how-to-sidestep-negative-thinking-patterns/

How to tell your friend they've hurt you. (n.d.). Friendships | ReachOut Australia. Retrieved October 14, 2022, from https://au.reachout.com/articles/how-to-tell-your-friend-theyve-hurt-you

How To Trigger Your Relaxation Response. (2020, March 12). Verywell Mind. Retrieved October 14, 2022, from https://www.verywellmind.com/what-is-the-relaxation-response-3145145

How To Trigger Your Relaxation Response. (2020b, March 12). Verywell Mind. Retrieved October 14, 2022, from https://www.verywellmind.com/what-is-the-relaxation-response-3145145

"image: Freepik.com". This cover has been designed using assets from Freepik.com

Is Journaling an Effective Stress Management Tool? (2020, March 27). Verywell Mind. Retrieved October 14, 2022, from https://www.verywellmind.com/the-benefits-of-journaling-for-stress-management-3144611

Is this a toxic friendship? (n.d.). Retrieved October 14, 2022, from https://au.reachout.com/toxic-friendship-quiz

Just a moment. . . (n.d.). Retrieved October 14, 2022, from https://www.mind.org.uk/information-support/types-of-mental-health-problems/self-esteem/tips-to-improve-your-self-esteem/

Just a moment. . . (n.d.-b). Retrieved October 14, 2022, from https://www.mind.org.uk/information-support/types-of-mental-health-problems/self-esteem/about-self-esteem/

Just a moment. . . (n.d.-c). Retrieved October 14, 2022, from https://www.indeed.com/career-advice/career-development/how-to-start-conversation-with-strangers

K, S. (2022, September 8). 6 Reasons Why People Fish For Compliments (and How to Respond). Aisles of Life. Retrieved October 14, 2022, from https://aislesoflife.com/2021/09/06/why-people-fish-for-compliments-and-how-to-respond/

Managing Panic Disorder With Positive Affirmations. (2020, June 24). Verywell Mind. Retrieved October 14, 2022, from https://www.verywellmind.com/positive-affirmations-for-stress-relief-3144809

Miller, K. (2021, November 18). 12 Tips for How To End a Conversation Instead of Dying a Thousand Deaths in Moments of Awkward Silence. Well+Good. Retrieved October 14, 2022, from https://www.wellandgood.com/how-to-end-conversation/

mindbodygreen. (2021, June 28). 10 Expert-Backed Tips To Help You Have Better Conversations. Mindbodygreen. Retrieved October 14, 2022, from https://www.mindbodygreen.com/articles/how-to-keep-conversation-going-10-tips-for-texting-and-more

mindbodygreen. (2021a, June 25). Are You In A Codependent Friendship? Here Are 8 Signs That You May Be. Mindbodygreen. Retrieved October 14, 2022, from https://www.mindbodygreen.com/articles/codependent-friendship-signs

mindbodygreen. (2021b, June 25). Are You In A Codependent Friendship? Here Are 8 Signs That You May Be. Mindbodygreen. Retrieved October 14, 2022, from https://www.mindbodygreen.com/articles/codependent-friendship-signs

mindbodygreen. (2021b, June 28). 11 Qualities Of A Good Friend & The Types Of "Friends" To Avoid. Mindbodygreen. Retrieved October 14, 2022, from https://www.mindbodygreen.com/articles/how-to-be-a-good-friend

mindbodygreen. (2021c, June 28). 11 Qualities Of A Good Friend & The Types Of "Friends" To Avoid. Mindbodygreen. Retrieved October 14, 2022, from https://www.mindbodygreen.com/articles/how-to-be-a-good-friend

Moore, C. P. (2022, September 12). Positive Daily Affirmations: Is There Science Behind It? PositivePsychology.com. Retrieved October 14, 2022, from https://positivepsychology.com/daily-affirmations/

Morin, D. A., B.Sc., S. B. V. A., B.Sc., S. B. V. A., Morin, D. A., Morin, D. A., Morin, D. A., Morin, D. A., Morin, D. A., Morin, D. A., & Morin, D. A. (2022, June 29). How To Become Friends With Someone Over Text. SocialSelf. Retrieved October 14, 2022, from https://socialself.com/blog/become-friends-text/

Morin, D. A., B.Sc., S. B. V. A., B.Sc., S. B. V. A., Morin, D. A., Morin, D. A., Morin, D. A., Morin, D. A., Morin, D. A., Morin, D. A., & Morin, D. A. (2022b, September 21). How to Become Friends With Someone (Fast). SocialSelf. Retrieved October 14, 2022, from https://socialself.com/blog/worlds-fastest-way-to-become-friends/

Morin, D. A., Morin, D. A., B.Sc., S. B. V. A., B.Sc., S. B. V. A., Morin, D. A., Morin, D. A., Morin, D. A., & Morin, D. A. (2022, August 5). Stuck in a One-Sided Friendship? Why & What to Do. SocialSelf. Retrieved October 14, 2022, from https://socialself.com/blog/one-sided-friendship/
Morin, D. A., Morin, D. A., B.Sc., S. B. V. A., B.Sc., S. B. V. A., Morin, D. A., Morin, D. A., Morin, D. A., & Morin, D. A. (2022, August 5). Stuck in a One-Sided Friendship? Why & What to Do. SocialSelf. Retrieved October 14, 2022, from https://socialself.com/blog/one-sided-friendship/

Morin, D. A., Morin, D. A., Morin, D. A., B.Sc., S. B. V. A., Morin, D. A., & B.Sc., S. B. V. A. (2022, August 31). Our top 3 tips on how to keep a conversation going. SocialSelf. Retrieved October 14, 2022, from https://socialself.com/blog/the-5-best-ways-to-keep-a-conversation-going/

Nguyen, Q. (2022, May 9). Teach kids 10 social media etiquette before posting anything. CyberPurify. Retrieved October 14, 2022, from https://cyberpurify.com/knowledge/10-social-media-etiquette-for-teens/

Nickalls, S. (2014, September 2). The 18 Unwritten Rules of Texting You Should Know. Lifehack. Retrieved October 14, 2022, from https://www.lifehack.org/articles/communication/the-18-unwritten-rules-texting-you-should-know.html

Nonverbal Communication and Body Language. (n.d.). HelpGuide.org. Retrieved October 14, 2022, from https://www.helpguide.org/articles/relationships-communication/nonverbal-communication.htm

Nunez, K. (2020, January 13). 3 Ways to Meditate for Better Sleep. Healthline. Retrieved October 14, 2022, from https://www.healthline.com/health/meditation-for-sleep
6 Polite Ways To End a Conversation. (2022, August 8). Southern Living. Retrieved October 14, 2022, from https://www.southernliving.com/culture/how-to-end-conversation-etiquette

Positive Self Talk for a Better Life. (2022, May 24). Verywell Mind. Retrieved October 14, 2022, from https://www.verywellmind.com/how-to-use-positive-self-talk-for-stress-relief-3144816

psycom.net. (n.d.). Retrieved October 14, 2022, from https://www.psycom.net/relationships/toxic-friendship-signs

Raypole, C. (2020, April 28). How to Become the Boss of Your Emotions. Healthline. Retrieved October 14, 2022, from https://www.healthline.com/health/how-to-control-your-emotions

Raypole, C. (2020b, May 19). In a Toxic Friendship? Here's What to Look For (and How to Handle It). Healthline. Retrieved October 14, 2022, from https://www.healthline.com/health/toxic-friendships

Raypole, C. (2020c, May 19). In a Toxic Friendship? Here's What to Look For (and How to Handle It). Healthline. Retrieved October 14, 2022, from https://www.healthline.com/health/toxic-friendships

5 Self-Care Practices for Every Area of Your Life. (2022, May 23). Verywell Mind. Retrieved October 14, 2022, from https://www.verywellmind.com/self-care-strategies-overall-stress-reduction-3144729

5 Self-Care Practices for Every Area of Your Life. (2022b, May 23). Verywell Mind. Retrieved October 14, 2022, from https://www.verywellmind.com/self-care-strategies-overall-stress-reduction-3144729

Self-esteem: Take steps to feel better about yourself. (2022, July 6). Mayo Clinic. Retrieved October 14, 2022, from https://www.mayoclinic.org/healthy-lifestyle/adult-health/in-depth/self-esteem/art-20045374?reDate=14102022

Self-Motivation: Definition, Examples, and Tips. (n.d.). The Berkeley Well-Being Institute. Retrieved October 14, 2022, from https://www.berkeleywellbeing.com/self-motivation.html

5 Simple Steps to Assertive Communication. (2020, February 13). Verywell Mind. Retrieved October 14, 2022, from https://www.verywellmind.com/learn-assertive-communication-in-five-simple-steps-3144969

Sinay, D. (2016, September 14). How to Make Friends in High School. Teen Vogue. Retrieved October 14, 2022, from https://www.teenvogue.com/gallery/how-to-make-friends-in-high-school-shy

Skipper, C. (2021, June 4). Katy Milkman Interview: How to Actually Change Your Behavior for the Better. GQ. Retrieved October 14, 2022, from https://www.gq.com/story/how-to-change-katy-milkman-interview

Somerville, C. (2020, March 2). 10 Bad Social Habits That Are Keeping You From Making Friends. ConvoConnection. Retrieved October 14, 2022, from https://www.convoconnection.com/blog/10-bad-social-habits-that-are-keeping-you-from-making-friends

Stanborough, R. M. J. (2019, December 18). What Are Cognitive Distortions and How Can You Change These Thinking Patterns? Healthline. Retrieved October 14, 2022, from https://www.healthline.com/health/cognitive-distortions

3 steps to better communication. (n.d.). ReachOut Australia. Retrieved October 14, 2022, from https://au.reachout.com/articles/3-steps-to-better-communication

The Beginning. . .. (2017, February 8). Journey to Self Esteem. Retrieved October 14, 2022, from https://journeytoselfesteem.wordpress.com/2017/01/24/the-beginning/

The Best Small Talk Questions to Ask When You Have SAD. (2020, November 12). Verywell Mind. Retrieved October 14, 2022, from https://www.verywellmind.com/how-do-i-ask-follow-up-questions-during-small-talk-3024865

The Fight-or-Flight Response Prepares Your Body to Take Action. (2022, September 21). Verywell Mind. Retrieved October 14, 2022, from https://www.verywellmind.com/what-is-the-fight-or-flight-response-2795194

The Role of Body Language in Communication - MCIS Language Solutions. (2022, July 20). Certified Translator Toronto, Translation Agency Toronto - MCIS Languages. Retrieved October 14, 2022, from https://www.mcislanguages.com/the-role-of-body-language-in-communication/

Thompson, M. (2021, December 16). The Shy Person's Guide to Starting Conversations with Strangers. Medium. Retrieved October 14, 2022, from https://medium.com/personal-growth/the-shy-persons-guide-to-starting-conversations-with-strangers-ea67f506c439

Thompson, M. (2022, January 13). How to Break the Ice and Start Conversations | Better Humans. Medium. Retrieved October 14, 2022, from https://betterhumans.pub/the-completely-audacious-guide-to-breaking-the-ice-3f6ea9bbac8d

Three Tricks for Starting a Conversation With a Stranger. (2022, March 23). Verywell Mind. Retrieved October 14, 2022, from https://www.verywellmind.com/how-to-start-a-conversation-with-a-stranger-3024391

10 Tips to Help You Make Friends and Get Along with Others. (n.d.). Retrieved October 14, 2022, from https://www.betterup.com/blog/10-tips-to-help-you-make-friends-and-get-along-better-with-others?hsLang=en

8 Ways Social Anxiety Changes the Way You Think About Everything. (2021, February 17). Verywell Mind. Retrieved October 14, 2022, from https://www.verywellmind.com/how-social-anxiety-changes-what-you-think-4088151

3 ways to end a toxic friendship. (n.d.). ReachOut Australia. Retrieved October 14, 2022, from https://au.reachout.com/articles/3-ways-to-end-a-toxic-friendship

What Are the Qualities of a Good Friend? 11 Characteristics. (n.d.). Retrieved October 14, 2022, from https://www.betterup.com/blog/qualities-of-a-good-friend

What Are the Signs of Healthy or Low Self-Esteem? (2022, October 10). Verywell Mind. Retrieved October 14, 2022, from https://www.verywellmind.com/what-is-self-esteem-2795868

What Having a "Growth Mindset" Actually Means. (2022, August 24). Harvard Business Review. Retrieved October 14, 2022, from https://hbr.org/2016/01/what-having-a-growth-mindset-actually-means

What Is Mindfulness? Does It Help Anxiety, Depression, or OCD? (2021, September 12). Manhattan Center for Cognitive Behavioral Therapy. Retrieved October 14, 2022, from https://www.manhattancbt.com/mindfulness/

What makes a good friend? (n.d.). Friendships | ReachOut Australia. Retrieved October 14, 2022, from https://au.reachout.com/articles/what-makes-a-good-friend

What makes a good friend? (n.d.-b). Retrieved October 14, 2022, from https://www.kidscape.org.uk/advice/advice-for-young-people/friendships-and-frenemies/what-makes-a-good-friend/

What's My Mindset? (n.d.). Retrieved October 14, 2022, from https://blog.mindsetworks.com/what-s-my-mindset

Williams, A. (2020, September 8). 7 strategies to help teens master social media etiquette. SmartSign Blog. Retrieved October 14, 2022, from https://www.smartsign.com/blog/7-strategies-help-teens-master-social-media-etiquette/

Made in the USA
Monee, IL
01 August 2024

63106028R00103